FOLLOWING
THE
Anointing

PART I

Donald R. Tredway, MD, PhD
and
Donna J. Tredway, RN

Following the Anointing: Part I
© 2024 by Donald R. Tredway and Donna J. Tredway

Published by Insight International, Inc.
contact@freshword.com
www.freshword.com
918-493-1718

Unless otherwise noted all Scripture quotations are taken from the New American Standard Bible. Copyright 1960, 1962, 1963, 1968, 1971, 1972, 1973, 1975, 1977 The Lockman Foundation, La Habra, CA. All rights reserved.

Scripture quotations marked (AMP) are taken from the Amplified Bible, Copyright 1978 by the Lockman Foundation, La Habra, CA. All rights reserved.

Scripture quotation marked (MSG) is taken from The Message: The New Testament, Psalms, and Proverbs. Copyright 1993, 1994, 1995, 1996, 2000, 2001, 2002 by Eugene H Peterson, NavPress Publishing Group.

ISBN: 978-1-960452-05-4
E-Book ISBN: 978-1-960452-06-1

Library of Congress Control Number: 2023921260

Printed in the United States of America.

Endorsements

This is a challenging and inspiring book as it traces Don's journey, together with Donna, on a spiritual journey that embraces an amazing personal healing and a life devoted to the Risen Savior.

Don's walk with the Lord has taken him to many countries and his quiet ministry in the Power of the Holy Spirit was a great blessing throughout our FGBMFI chapters in Australia with many lives delivered from satanic oppression and the wonderful moving of the gifts of the Spirit in the meetings.

— *David Grantham*
National Director, FGBMFI, Australia

The part of Dr. Don Tredway's story that I knew prior to reading this book inspired me. I wanted more of what he had. But reading this book inspired me so much more. My own hunger for more of the anointing has grown much larger as I've read about how God has worked with and through him in fascinating, powerful, and surprising ways. I know Dr. Tredway; these stories are real. I believe you will be enriched and inspired in reading this also. May the anointing touch your heart and life as you give God through His Holy Spirit permission to do all He desires to do with and through you.

— *Carol Tanksley*, MD, DMin
Author of *Overcoming Fear and Anxiety Through Spiritual Warfare*
and *The Christian's Journey Through Grief*

I have known Dr. Don and "More Than a Doctor" Donna for almost forty years. However, it has been a thrilling journey to walk with them through the record of their "Following the Anointing." I was deeply impressed by how Part 1 of their journey finishes with Don's deep revelation of the Father's love for him and his being securely established as a truly beloved son. Again, a clear testimony of God's willingness to include us in what He is doing when there are works that He sees still need to be done in our lives.

Don and Donna's willingness to step out of the familiar, secure, and comfortable into the unknown is met with the Lord's capacity of being able to take an inch of our availability, then turning it into a mile of grace for us and blessing to many. My time of being ministered to by Don and Donna established my understanding of the importance of the need in the whole human race to be embraced. Dr. Baxter Kruger, author of *God Is for us,* says that Paul's true sense in Ephesians 1:6 is that we have been embraced in the Beloved. Through and in Christ the Father has fully embraced us. Yet, as the Tredways found, there are many who have no memory of being embraced. My time with Don and Donna ministering into the void in my person of that need for bonding at birth has made me aware of the importance of being available to the Spirit as a human agent to embrace the unembraceable.

I saw this not long after my time of being ministered to on the Kona Campus. I was walking right near the area where the Tredways had their DTS lectures. It had now been turned into a dining area. I noticed a guy on my left as I was passing. I had a clear impression that I should go over and give him a hug. He immediately broke down and wept. He collapsed into my arms, and after a while I wondered how long this would last and was reminded how long

Donna just held me in a motherly embrace. He was so grateful and simply said, "I just needed that right now."

On another occasion, leaning into Donna's initiative, I was made aware that my mother-in-law did not have a lot of time left before she would pass. I had been trying to draw her to Jesus for over forty years. I got the distinct impression that I should ask for a special time with her and that I was to explain to her that the Father had already reached out to embrace her in and through Jesus. All that was required by her was to respond to His embrace. When I arrived at the nursing home she was in her favorite chair. I explained that I would kneel before her and embrace her as the Father would and that I would lead her in a prayer of embracing His embrace. The next days the nurses in the home remarked on the amazing transformation in her life. I can only explain that as the continuing miracle of grace through Donna's example of "Following the Anointing."

— *Tom Hallas*
Elder Asia Pacific
Former Field Director, Asia Pacific
Youth With A Mission

Contents

Foreword

Perhaps it was the finely tooled cowboy boots, perhaps the engaging smile, or maybe his infectious sense of humor. But something drew me to Dr. Don Tredway from the moment we met. As a young physician, I began to understand that here was a man who could help me resolve many of the spiritual issues with which I had wrestled for years.

I was privileged to introduce him to Australian healthcare professionals and later traveled widely with him in China where I began to understand his trust and dependency on Father God and his deep relationship with the Holy Spirit.

In this, the first of a two-part series, Don tells of his early experience as a doctor, academic, teacher, and naval officer. He tells of his transition from nominal Christianity to one who was transformed by the miraculous healing power of God.

The book is divided into two parts. The first is a narrative where Don and his wife, Donna, relate their growing understanding of what it means to live in Christ by the power of God's Holy Spirit.

Issues dealt with include hearing the voice of God, understanding the unconditional love and the Father-heart of God, dealing with spiritual opposition, and the awareness that all spiritual experiences must be Bible-based.

The second comprises appendices containing detailed teaching on such subjects as the character of God, principles of inner healing, and the nature of sin and deliverance. This section will serve as a reference and be of immense value to those seeking a deeper life in the Spirit of God.

Following the Anointing Part 1 by Donald and Donna Tredway is a book for Christians at all stages of maturity and for those who are yet to find the peace and fulfillment that only a saving relationship with Jesus Christ can bring.

— *Dr. Ernest Frank Crocker*, BSc (Med)
MBBS FRACP DDU FAANMS
New South Wales Chair, Christian Medical
and Dental Fellowship of Australia

Acknowledgments

To our four daughters, who have walked through some of these experiences with us.

We also want to acknowledge all the people who have prayed for us and financially supported us.

I, Don, want to also thank my wife, Donna, for standing beside me all these years. Her support and encouragement were instrumental in my journey with the Lord. This is also a part of her story in "Following the Anointing" of the Lord in her own life. Quite often she would stay in the background, leaving the public ministry to me while she ministered one on one. The depth of her ministry and discernment is profound and a witness to me (as mentioned also by Tom Hallas). The anointing of the Lord is so much stronger during the times we are ministering together. In addition to her inserts in this book, I appreciate her editing skills of my verbose nature.

Finally, both Donna and I want to acknowledge the faithfulness of God and thank Him for revealing Himself to us in a very tangible and meaningful way as we tried to follow His voice.

Introduction

This is the initial portion of the path that my wife, Donna, and I have had in following our Lord Jesus Christ. This story will show not only our failures, struggles, and pain but also the faithfulness and loving-kindness of God. It is not our intention to write about ourselves, but about the Lord and His anointing that is available to all obedient servants who walk with Him. To that end, we will share, along with others, in what they observed and our various perspectives as to what the Lord has done in our lives and others through His anointing. As you read, let faith grow in your heart. Seek His face, be transformed by the Holy Spirit (HS), and let God's glory be manifest in you. Let this book encourage you to grow in the Lord and allow the Holy Spirit to guide you in taking others into God's presence. Following Him releases tremendous joy, peace, and love along with challenges. I pray that you will come to a new understanding of God the Father and His tremendous love for each one of us. As you become secure in Him and know Him as Abba Father, you will be released into all that He has for you.

Come walk with us through this first part of our journey as we learned to follow the Lord and His Holy Spirit. He initially led me from the practice of medicine to a period of full-time ministry with total dependence upon Him for myself and my family. Then as I became secure in Him, He had me return to medicine and a marketplace ministry (part two of our journey).

CHAPTER 1

Road to *Damascus* Experience

Proverbs 4:20-22 My son, give attention to my words; incline your ear to my sayings. Do not let them depart from your sight; keep them in the midst of your heart. For they are life to those who find them and health to all their body.

Just like Luke, the beloved physician who was a follower and servant of Jesus, my life was changed when I encountered the wonderful power of God. It did not come without a struggle. In the mid-1970s I was stationed at the Naval Hospital in Oakland, California, and still remember the day I walked into my Navy orthopedic surgeon's office and was told that I would never be able to work as a physician again and that I would be discharged from the Navy with a total disability. Three years prior I had undergone a successful laminectomy for a herniated lumbar disc. A year later I had another herniated lumbar disc, but this time the surgery was unsuccessful, and I had an unstable back. To correct the problem, a lumbar fusion was performed that was given a 50% chance of being successful.

After this third surgery, I was in a plaster cast for six weeks. The cast went from my armpits to my knees and had a wooden pole that spread my legs. It was a very difficult time of hospital confinement. I was on the medical staff in the Department of Obstetrics and Gynecology, and the doctors in training under me would stop by for consultations. It helped break the boredom and gave me something to do. I read many books during that time and even began reading my Bible again. Even though I grew up in a Christian home and had accepted Jesus as my Savior, medicine became my major emphasis. I had accepted Jesus as a teenager at a Methodist Church camp and even felt the call to become a medical missionary. My parents were proud of me for going into medicine, although my father was not happy about the missionary part. I saw all my fourteen years of professional education dangling in the air as I lay there in bed.

After finishing medical school at the University of Illinois College of Medicine in Chicago, I completed a rotating internship at Great Lakes Naval Hospital in Great Lakes, Illinois. From there I went to Viet Nam as the squadron medical officer for COMLANSHIPRON 9 (LSTs and LSMRs) based in Yokosuka, Japan. A year later I was accepted into a three-year Navy training program in Obstetrics and Gynecology at the Naval Hospital in Portsmouth, Virginia. From there the Navy sent me to a three-year fellowship in Reproductive Endocrinology and Infertility at the University of Southern California in Los Angeles. There I earned a PhD degree in Physiology. After the subspecialty training, I was stationed at the Naval Hospital in Oakland, California, where I helped establish the first Navy training program in Reproductive Endocrinology and Infertility. Now as I look back at those times, I see the fulfillment of the scriptures "favor with God and favor with man" (**Luke 2:52** and **Psalm 5:12**), not knowing then what God had planned for me. During my training in Portsmouth, Captain Robert Baker was the chairman of the Department Ob/Gyn and took an interest in my family and my professional career. He was instrumental in my obtaining the Navy-sponsored fellowship. During my time in Portsmouth, he was promoted to one of the first Clinical Navy Admirals. Dr. Baker and his family became lifelong friends of our family. I thank the Lord for guiding my progress even when I did not recognize He was there.

Medicine became the center of my life, my family second, and God, who had called me to become a medical missionary, became third. In that hospital bed, as I opened my Bible, one scripture stood out and really spoke to me.

> Proverbs 4:20-22 My son, give attention to my words; incline your ear to my sayings. Do not let them depart from your sight; keep them in the midst of your heart. For they are life to those who find them and health to all their body.

"Give attention to my words" got my attention, but I had a hard time with the healing part. With all my medical and scientific training, I had to understand everything before I could accept it. Something happened to me in that hospital room when I prayed, "God, I trust You." With that, I had a peace that didn't make sense to my mind. This scripture became the foundation of my walk with God.

As I look back now, I can see how God was beginning to speak to me when I would listen, and excitement began to build as God opened doors. I was contacted by the University of Chicago and asked to come and interview for Section Chief of Reproductive Endocrinology in the Department of Obstetrics and Gynecology. As I prayed, I felt the Lord say to leave the security of the Navy after 12 years of active duty and to take the job.

After I came out of the hip spica plaster cast, I had to wear a fiberglass brace that went from under my arms down to the pelvis. During this time of recuperation, I had to fly to Chicago (November 1976) to take an oral exam for my Reproductive Endocrinology and Infertility Boards. Donna went with me, as I needed assistance because of having to use a cane and wearing the fiberglass brace. The plane ride was difficult, and as soon as we got to the hotel, I was on my back in bed for 8 hours on pain medication. When I had to get up and take the oral examination for the subspecialty, it was as if I had an extra strength, which I now know was from the Lord. I completed the exam successfully. (At that time there were only 40 of us in the world who had those credentials.)

While in Chicago, I interviewed at the University of Chicago and was offered a tenured (position guaranteed for life) professorship as the Head of Reproductive Endocrinology and Infertility in the Department of Obstetrics and Gynecology with a dual appointment in the Department of Internal Medicine Endocrinology Section. I was very excited because this was what I had been working for my whole academic life, and God was leading me there. I was still weak, but every day I grew stronger physically. This new position was dependent upon my being physically well. I was in my mid-30s and had my whole life ahead of me. God was with me. I began planning to leave the service.

We were shown around Chicago, and one Sunday on a return trip to Chicago to look for a house, we wanted to go to Moody Bible Church. We took public transportation and got lost looking for the church. As we were standing on a corner, someone came up to us and said, "Are you looking for Moody Church?" We said yes and he gave us directions. As we started to go that way, we turned to thank him, and he was gone. This was one of our angel experiences and again confirmed that the Lord was leading us to Chicago.

Donna: The following is a story that I wrote about what happened that Sunday morning at Moody.

On Sunday morning, May 8th, 1977, Don and I attended morning services at Moody Bible Institute in Chicago. When the service was over, we went to the visitors' reception and from there on to a tour of the facilities. Not until we reached the second to the last room did I notice a middle-aged man in his 50s, dressed in black except for a white shirt. The thing that drew my attention to him was a Star of David tiepin which to me covered his whole chest (actually, it was an average size pin). I went to him and placed my finger on it and asked if he was a "completed" Jew. I couldn't make out his answer as it seemed muffled. The tour went into the main sanctuary, and for some reason I was drawn to this man and felt the need to tag along with him instead of my husband. In the sanctuary, the eyes of this Jew fell on a beautiful grand piano. As he stroked it, he told me the piano's kind and of its value. In our conversation he told me that he had once been a concert pianist and was interested in music. He told me that he was a Levite and was an assistant rabbi from Louisville, Kentucky. Putting later conversations together at the time of this writing, his whole life seemed to have been devoted to his religion and God. He had spent seven years in college, was fluent in Hebrew, knew Greek, was well versed in Old Testament scriptures, had handwritten the Torah, visited and studied the Holy Land, and had studied Christ as a prophet—a well-learned fellow. While he was telling me these things my eyes could not leave the Star of David that was "plastered" all over his chest. I again put my finger on it and asked if he was a Christian Jew. He said that he was not but had come to Moody to hear a choral group that he thought was to sing that morning. (As it turned out, the group was to sing for the evening service.) By now I wasn't aware of the tour group, and the only thing I could think to do was to pull the "I FOUND IT AND YOU CAN FIND IT TOO" pamphlet from my purse. As soon as I did Satan said, "Put that away! He can't understand that. That was written for gentiles not Jews." I put it away. He went on to say how he loved God and was seeking a real relationship with Him. He also said that while he was there at Moody, he would like to have a discussion with one of the ministers. I was really bewildered because I knew no one there. Another voice said to me, "Take out the pamphlet." I did so, and when my friend told me again how he really desired a personal relationship with God, I suddenly said, "But you can." I pulled him into a short hall and began to invisibly diagram on a wall how God was separated from man by sin and that by no amount of work or religion can God be reached. I went on to tell him that it is only through the Messiah, Jesus Christ, the Sacrificial Holy Lamb of God, that man can reach Him and that it is the Messiah who bridges the gap between man and God. At that point, he said that if he believed that his friends would nail him to a cross. I believe that what the Holy Spirit had me say next started the veil over his spiritual eyes to lift. I reminded him that according to Hebrew beliefs, a man's soul does not leave the body until the third day. I reminded him that Jesus was dead for three days before reappearing to man, and according to Jewish law had to have been dead. I asked him if he had ever studied or read the last part of Isaiah 52 and the 53rd chapter. He went on to tell me that of all the scriptures he had studied, the 52nd chapter was the one he had never been able to understand. I explained that the reason he was not able to understand was because there was a veil separating knowledge from truth. I went on to say that because the Jews, having been the chosen people of God, rejected Him, God turned His back on them. I said that not only is there a veil from God, but Satan didn't want him to see and that he confused, twisted, or did anything else in his power to prevent him from seeing the truth. At that point, my husband walked by, and I asked him to find me a Bible (we had forgotten ours at the hotel). He did so and left. I read passages from the I FOUND IT pamphlet (New Testament passages) and immediately his mind would flash to Old Testament verses that correlated. He recited them in Hebrew, then in English, and then would look them up in the scriptures and read them. I then took my friend into another room where we sat down, and I asked him to start reading the last verses from Isaiah 52 through the 53rd chapter. As he did so you could see the veil begin to lift from his eyes, and almost as suddenly, the veil would fall. He would grab his chest and say, "You don't know what's going on inside me; the turmoil I'm in." Several times while reading these chapters he confessed to the turmoil, and I could see physically the "fight" that was going on within him. As he would read, tears started coming into his eyes. I grabbed him in my arms, held him tight, and prayed that God would somehow help him to see the truth. Almost immediately the veil was lifted, and he had instant insight into things of the Spirit—it was beautiful. He suddenly realized that in his Jewish religion, there was no way for God to forgive their sins because there was no more animal sacrifice, and he realized the significance of a blood sacrifice. He explained how when a lamb was sacrificed the priests would lay their hands upon it to transfer the sins of the people to the lamb. I explained how the weight of our sins, past, present, and future, were placed upon Christ on the cross. He went on to describe the slaughter and the bleeding, and instantly he could see the blood of Jesus running over Him (remember that this man had studied Christ but only as a prophet). Instantly my friend saw Jesus as the Messiah and revealed how Christ never uttered an evil word and that the only time He spoke during His trial was only in response to truths spoken.

When the truth was revealed to him, my friend rocked back and forth in his chair sobbing from deep within, almost falling out of his chair, and repeated, "He is the Messiah. He is the Messiah." As we sat there, David, my friend, took me on a tour of the Tabernacle and explained the symbolism of the furnishings and ceremonies and how they all pointed to Jesus—how thrilling it was.

When we left the room, we walked through the sanctuary and David went to the grand piano and started playing Handel's Messiah. As he played, he wept as he realized more and more the truth about Jesus. My friend, Don, and I were the only ones in the sanctuary, and the presence of God filled the place as David played.

Whenever there is a victory for God there always is a backlash from Satan. This joyful event was no exception. The janitor came in and told David to stop playing the piano. I tried to explain to the janitor what had just happened, but he was adamant that the piano was off-limits and that he had to quit. I can still recall the coldness of the room when God's tangible presence left. The three of us left Moody together. Out in front of the church, Don and I walked off in one direction and David in another. We had no idea where he was staying or how to get ahold of him. He too was just visiting the city.

Several months later our family moved to Chicago. I started praying that somehow we would be able to come across David's path again. I called Moody Bible Institute and explained who I was and what happened at the church and asked if anyone saw this man if they would contact me. I can't remember right now how long it was, but I did get a phone call from someone at the church stating that they had seen him there. I was able to eventually locate him and brought him to our house to stay with us during his visit back to Chicago. He told me many things about his life and how he had been abused and hated by his father as a child. He had never experienced the love and acceptance that we had in our home, and it was overpowering for him. He had to leave. We never saw David again but did receive several postcards from him briefly talking about doing God's work in the streets of New York. Our family moved from Chicago, and he had no way to find us again.

It has been many years since I have told the story of David. I don't know what happened to him. At times I would be burdened to pray for him, but that hasn't happened now for many years, and I feel that he is probably with the Lord. I do know that he felt called to the Jews in New York City and at one time had a street ministry there.

I feel so privileged and honored to have been used in David's life. I have seen God do many miracles, but being chosen to bring this Jewish rabbi to the Lord, for me, has so far been the highlight of all.

Don: I returned to the Naval Hospital in Oakland, California, and began working half days doing mainly paperwork and eventually saw a few outpatients. I was excited when my physician finally took me out of the brace and when I was able to do surgery again. One day as I was ending an abdominal hysterectomy procedure, the old pain returned. Before I knew it, I was back on pain medication and was only able to sit for short periods of time. It was at that time the orthopedic surgeon told me I would be discharged from the Navy with a total disability and not be able to work again. Here I thought the Lord was speaking to me to go to the University of Chicago, but there was no way that that could happen physically. I had already submitted my Navy resignation papers since I was convinced that God was speaking to me. There was no way that I could accept the position. I figured what my disability income would be, and it would not support my family's (four daughters and wife) current lifestyle, let alone pay our mortgage. I was very discouraged and depressed. My whole life was falling apart.

I remembered at that time Donna telling me about a healing service she had gone to while visiting a friend, Carol Rhodes, in Southern California.

Donna: In the first part of 1977, a friend from the LA area came to visit us in the Bay Area of San Francisco. He shared with us that Carol had had an encounter with God that lasted for a week and was now praying in tongues. That intrigued me, and I wanted to know more about her experience. I, along with another mutual friend, went to visit Carol to hear more about that event. She explained that she had been baptized in the Spirit and that we too could receive the baptism if we would just ask the Lord for it. That evening my friend and I got down on our knees and asked. My friend started shaking and crying as she experienced the infilling, but I had no reaction whatsoever. I received it by faith and thanked the Lord for the gift.

Carol also shared that she was now going to a new church, Melodyland in Anaheim, and asked us to go with her to a healing service. The church had been a theater in the round and held several thousand people. It was packed. The music started and people began to praise God and lift their hands. It scared me so much that I wanted to run out. I had never heard or seen anything like that in my Presbyterian upbringing. I stayed and observed, felt awkward, and really wasn't sure what was happening. Then the pastor, Ralph Wilkerson, said, "We are going to have miracles of creation, and if there is anyone here who has never seen a miracle, I want you to come forward. There will be lengthening of legs." Well, I had never seen a miracle so I and one other person out of the several thousands of people there went forward to observe. Sure enough, a man sitting in a chair had one short leg, and when the pastor prayed, the leg grew out beyond the longer one and then came back to equalize the length of both legs. I took that story home and told Don that "he needed to go there to get fixed up."

Don: Needless to say, when Donna came home and shared that with me, I could not accept it because I could not explain it. For me, medicine was the only source of healing. Something else happened at that time. I was running a fellowship program in the US Navy for Reproductive Endocrinology and Infertility at the Oakland Naval Hospital and Metabolic Research Unit. There was a new surgical procedure, microsurgery, being taught in Anaheim, California, to which I was going to send my fellows. I was going to go along but not take the course because I could not operate. I wanted to get away and have a change of surroundings. While they attended the course, I was just going to rest. The venue for the course was not far from the church in Anaheim where Donna had gone. The church had a weekly healing service on Thursday mornings. In the middle of the night, I woke Donna and told her to call her friend and tell her that I wanted to go to the healing service.

Donna: Don woke me up around 2:00 AM and said that he would go to the church service and to call Carol in the morning. There was one big problem. Carol was on vacation at a resort someplace, but I had no idea where. I didn't know if it was in California, Arizona, or some other state. It came time for me to call, and I told the Lord that if He wanted Don to go to that service He would have to give me the phone number. I had no idea of the area code where they were so put in a three-number area code plus the business directory phone number 555-1212. When the operator answered (you could talk to a real person in those days), I said, "Look, I am trying to find some people, and I have absolutely no idea where they are. I know that they are at a resort area and it sounds something like costa quaza." She said, "Oh, you mean Coda de Casa. It is in (she gave me the name of the canyon, the county, and town) and the phone number is" and gave me the phone number. I about fell out of the chair I was sitting on. It had to have been an angel. I called the number and was able to get ahold of Carol.

Don: Of course, the next morning I couldn't believe that I had asked her to do that. I thought I must have taken too much codeine. At this time Donna and I went to a professional basketball game. A friend and I had bought season tickets for the Golden State Warriors. They were wonderful tickets, mid-court, four rows up. The Warriors were a good team that year, and I had not been able to go. I was miserable at the game and could only sit for twenty to thirty minutes at a time without getting up and walking and having to take pain medication. I never will forget, as we finally left the game and went to the car, we turned on the radio and a preacher was talking about healing. I decided to go to the healing service but made Donna promise not to tell anyone what I was going to do.

It is quite a process in the Navy going through a disability board review for active-duty members. It was during the review time that I flew to Southern California. I had difficulty traveling so I flew with a non-practicing Jewish obstetrician-gynecologist friend in his private plane along with a Buddhist and an agnostic obstetrician-gynecologist friend. At the airport in Anaheim, we were met by a Mormon OB/GYN friend. If you are going on a faith walk, it is important to surround yourself with men of faith, right? Of course, I did not share with them where I was planning to go the next day. On the first day of the meeting, after they left to go to the surgical course, I met our friend, Carol Rhodes, and went to the Thursday morning healing service at Melodyland Christian Center, a former theater in the round near Disneyland.

As the church service began, the congregation began singing, praising God, and lifting their hands. I became very uncomfortable because it was so different from anything I had ever experienced. There was a joy in the faces and voices of the people that I could not explain or understand. They were happy to be there on a Thursday morning. I had gone to church all my life out of tradition and obligation. I was disappointed because the regular minister, Ralph Wilkerson,[1] was delayed and one of the associate pastors started the service. That irritated me because I wanted to see Pastor Wilkerson as he supposedly had a healing ministry, whatever that was. However, the first thing the associate pastor said was that God was going to heal twenty people of back problems. That got my attention. Some people went forward. He prayed for them, and they fell to the floor. A while later they would get up and say that the pain was gone. I couldn't believe it. How I wanted to believe but I couldn't. Then the associate pastor had a word about stomach ulcers being healed. (I thought perhaps he was doing a review of systems like we do in medicine). A woman who was sitting on the aisle a few seats away from me stood up, lifted her hand, started shaking all over, and then fell to the floor. No one had touched her. "Oh my," I thought. "Are these the 'holy rollers' I heard about as a kid?" She eventually stood up and said she was healed. I facetiously thought, "Sure!"

Another woman went forward with a large goiter on her neck. He prayed for her, and it disappeared except for the floppy skin where the goiter was. I couldn't believe it for this was something that I could treat. It would take a few months of oral medication and then probably surgery, but it disappeared right in front of my eyes. I had not recovered from that when a nurse in uniform took an elderly man forward in a wheelchair. He must have had a CVA (stroke) for he was paralyzed in one arm and leg. The associate pastor prayed for him and his whole body shook (I thought the pastor was shaking his head). He stood up, took a couple of steps, and was unstable, but by the time he got to the top of the aisle, I could not tell anything was wrong with him. This just blew my mind because there was no way that I could explain that with all my medical knowledge except for the power of God. The people began to sing and praise God. Most unlike me, I joined in praising Him and thanking Him for what I had seen. For the first time in my life, I had seen the reality of Jesus Christ. I had seen the power of the resurrection.

Pastor Wilkerson finally arrived. He prayed against unbelief and prayed for the glory of God to fill the place. He then called for the exact number of people with back problems that had not gone forward from the original 20. Then he said, "The devil is defeated. Faith is determined. There are serious cases here in the service."

I went forward. I didn't see a minister; I saw the Lord Jesus Christ, and I just wanted to touch the hem of His garment. The ushers felt my brace. I told them what was wrong with me and that I was a physician. Wilkerson then said, "You are a doctor, and if God does it you will know it. Lord, we thank you for your doctors. I thank you for this doctor and the Spirit of God is all over your body, sir, from the top of your head to the soles of your feet. Thank God for this doctor everyone. Sir, you came a long way but not in vain. You have come in faith. God has done a work in you. I must hug you. Jesus, I praise You for this man; O God, You have put Your hand upon this man. You are calling him to a greater work. Lord, You've proven Yourself to him so many times. Lord, we have been waiting for a fulfillment of this miracle. Now, God, we praise You for resurrection power and I pray for healing up and down this body. He has braces all over his body. When were you filled with the Spirit? Yes, right now. You know everyone I praise God for physical healing, but the spiritual healing is so important. Lord, I pray that You will keep on filling this doctor, many fillings, go back and get more and more. In the name of Jesus, You are filling him with power. Let's just praise Jesus, and everyone begin praying in the Spirit. Lord, this man is filled with compassion, fill him more. Doctor, this is a new day for you. You have a lot ahead of you."

As soon as he put his hand on my forehead, I felt the most wonderful peace I have ever felt, and the constant pain in my left leg was gone. My left leg started jumping up and down, and I could not control it. I had no control over my body whatsoever. Then the one thing I had been so critical of happened to me. I fell to the floor under the power of God. After a short while, I got up and they ministered to me some more. It is hard to describe how you feel when the presence of God is in your body. There is a peace and love beyond understanding. As the congregation was praising God, I was also but they began praying in the Spirit while I was praying in English. I thought, "What is this, tongues?" I had been taught that didn't exist anymore as well as supernational healing, but I had just been healed. Pastor Wilkerson told me to stop praying in English and to pray without the understanding. I too began praying in the Spirit. After that, I went back to my seat. Something told me to go and take off my brace. I went to the restroom, took my brace off, and felt to see if the scar was still there. It was. I was disappointed, but I could bend over and touch my toes and there was no pain. I then walked back into the church service carrying my brace above my head, crying, praising the Lord.

Wilkerson called me forward saying, "Hello doctor, amen. I tell you something (while the people were clapping). As God is my witness, when I was praying for you, I was praying for a ministry to open up in your life. A ministry that will be tremendous. God has a plan, and He is going to use you. He is going to use you in so many ways and send so many people to you and use you in so many ways that you are going to tell God to slow down. Are you ready? In the name of Jesus, God, I am thanking You for the anointing that is on this man of God, set in the body of Christ, that the oil of the Holy Spirit will rest on his life, completed and given to Jesus. Lord, You have done a work in him today, and we give You praise. We give you praise; we give you praise; everyone give Him praise. To God give Him the glory! Everyone pray for this doctor; God is going to use him in a very special way."

I walked into that church service not believing in supernatural healing or the baptism of the Holy Spirit, and God accomplished both in my life that day. On that day, April 7, 1977, on Maud Thursday I came to a new understanding of Jesus Christ and His resurrection. I praise Him for the physical healing, but I praise Him more for what He did on the inside.

> Isaiah 30:18 (AMP) And therefore the Lord [earnestly] waits [expecting, looking, and longing] to be gracious to you; and therefore, He lifts Himself up, that He may have mercy on you and show loving-kindness to you. For the Lord is a God of justice. Blessed (happy, fortunate, to be envied) are all those who [earnestly] wait for Him, who expect and look and long for Him [for His victory, His favor, His love, His peace, His joy, and His matchless, unbroken companionship]!

I found out later that a prayer group from a small Methodist Church in Cerritos, California, was instrumental in my healing. This was a group of precious friends from the time I was at the University of Southern California doing my fellowship in Reproductive Endocrinology. Without my knowledge, they had been praying and doing a partial fast for my healing during the previous year.

The week after my healing, I mowed my yard. It had been a long time since I was able to do it. (I have gotten over that now. Donna does it.) My neighbor who used to help carry me out of our van and into the house when I went home for a visit in the hip spica cast, came out and wanted to know what happened. As I shared, he accepted the Lord Jesus Christ as his Savior in my yard. Another neighbor, a psychologist who also helped carry me into the house, also wanted to know what happened. As I shared, he also accepted the Lord.

Rev 12:11 'And they overcame him because of the blood of the Lamb and because of the word of their testimony.'

The next week I was back to work, operating and sharing what God had done. I walked into my orthopedic surgeon's office without my brace, bent over, and told him what God had done for me. He examined me, confirmed what had happened, and said, "You have a greater physician than me."

I wanted to share my miracle with everyone, but not everyone wanted to hear. Many avoided me. At times I would feel a twinge in my back, and I would wonder if the pain was coming back. I would then recall what had happened and would praise God. This twinge always seemed to occur just before someone wanted to know what happened to me. I resigned from the Navy after twelve years of active duty and accepted a position at the University of Chicago. What did God have for me now?

I have a cassette recording of that healing service. As I listen to it and recall the experience as I write this part of my journey, God brought the following scripture to mind:

I John 2:20 (AMP) But you have an anointing from the Holy One [you have been set apart, specially gifted, and prepared by the Holy Spirit], and all of you know [the truth because He teaches us, illuminates our minds, and guards us from error].

I believe the Lord wants to encourage you in what He has called you to do. Has He spoken similar words to you and appointed a work for you to do? I want to encourage you to follow His anointing and to let the Holy Spirit guide and teach you. You may fall at times, just as we have, but He will always pick you up. Do not miss what God has for you!

Don and Donna on honeymoon, 1964

Lt. Tredway, Navy Photo, 1966

*Staff and residents at
Oakland Naval Hospital, 1977,
shortly after Dr. Tredway's healing.
(Dr. Tredway, first row, kneeling far left.)*

*LCDR Tredway and Donna 1968,
Portsmouth, VA*

CHAPTER 2

The Aftermath
in *Chicago*

Acts 22:15 For you will be a witness for Him to all men of what you have seen and heard.

It was exciting to return to the city where Donna and I met (she was in nursing school and I was in medical school) although I had forgotten about the winters. The University of Chicago (U of C) was in the south side of Chicago in a depressed area, so we chose to live in the southern suburb of Flossmoor. The public schools in Flossmoor were very progressive in individualization and liberty for the students. We felt our four daughters needed a more structured environment, so we enrolled them in the Christian school where we attended church (Homewood Full Gospel Church). I was later asked, and accepted, to be on the church school board. Homewood was an independent church where the Lord exposed us to the gifts of the Spirit. Sometimes it seemed to us to be in excess.

Donna: I thought that the church services at Melodyland were far from my Presbyterian upbringing, but this Full Gospel Church had Melodyland beat. I for sure wanted out of there the first time we went. The gifts of the Spirit were in full operation, and it scared me because I had no understanding of what was happening. I had never had any teaching in the church on the Holy Spirit or His gifts even though He was mentioned along with God the Father and Son. I was dumbfounded to learn that the Holy Spirit was a "person."

Although I wasn't comfortable at that Full Gospel Church, "something" kept drawing us back. God began to deal with me and began to teach me about the third person of the Trinity and His character.

Don: For me, adjusting to being in full-time academia was exciting. I met Nobel laureates, had lunch in the Faculty Club, and participated in a research program. I was a tenured associate professor, had a secured position, and our children would have been able to go to any university in the United States and have their tuition paid for by the University of Chicago up to the amount of its tuition. I was so proud of what I had accomplished. One day when I was having lunch in the Faculty Club, God spoke to me from

> **Colossians 2:8,9:** See to it that no one takes you captive through philosophy and empty deception, according to the tradition of men, according to the elementary principles of the world, rather than according to Christ.

I had forgotten that it was the Lord who had given me all those things and that He was the source of all knowledge.

Intellectually, the University of Chicago was stimulating. I established a section of Reproductive Endocrinology and Infertility and had a joint appointment in the Department of Internal Medicine where we had joint research projects in infertility. Academically, this was one of the most fulfilling times of my professional life.

While I enjoyed my academic life, family life was difficult. I got up early in the morning to take the train to work before the children and Donna were up and arrived home after the children were in bed. The Department also had teaching sessions for residents and students on Saturday morning, which meant that I only had a half day off Saturday and all day Sunday to be with the family. Chicago for Donna was a desert experience since she was alone most of the time. This became a concern and prayer item for me. I felt I was out of balance for my children and wife.

Our time at Homewood Full Gospel Church challenged our Methodist and Presbyterian backgrounds. As I read about the ministry of John Wesley (founder of the Methodist Church), I noticed that the same gifts that were in operation at our church were in operation during the time of his ministry. I was never taught about that in my Methodist catechism classes as a young man. No wonder the spiritual gifts of the Holy Spirit are missing in many churches today.

Our church had a monthly men's breakfast and time of prayer and worship. One Saturday I took the group to the University of Chicago's Faculty Club building. I believe we had spiritual breakthroughs in the heavenlies that day. As we were worshiping, one of the Faculty Club employees came and closed our door to the hallway to decrease the sound to the rest of the building. Isn't that just like the enemy?

I thanked God for the things He was revealing to me through the Holy Spirit and even began to pray for my patients before surgery.

My spiritual growth through the church was exciting. I would read multiple books on healing and the baptism of the Holy Spirit and would sit in my study at home and try to pray in the Spirit again, but nothing would happen. I would read more books and get more frustrated. This continued for approximately six months. One day as I was worshiping and thanking God for who He is, I began praying in the Spirit again. I was still having a battle with my mind.

I had medical meetings in the Los Angeles area during the next few years and would adjust my schedule to return to Melodyland for our family to attend the annual charismatic conference. It was during those times that I became acquainted with Pastor Ralph Wilkerson and his wife, Eileen. He became my spiritual father.

I would often be asked to share my testimony in local churches in the Chicago area. I will never forget one Sunday at a suburban Chicago church where I shared my testimony and then sat down. The pastor got up and said, "If anyone wants Dr. Tredway to pray for you for healing, come forward." I almost fell out of my chair because I had never been asked to or prayed for anyone to be healed. I prayed, but in an unsettled manner.

That situation really brought things to the surface for me. There was no doubt in my mind that God could heal, but it was for ministers to do the praying, not me. Also, at that time I received a letter from my neighbor in California who had accepted the Lord on my lawn after I shared the testimony. He shared how God was using him to pray for the sick. I asked the Lord why Rick was able to move in healing, but I was not. Then I realized the meaning of **Rev 12:11 (the power of one's testimony)** and **Mark 16:17-18 (lay hands on the sick and they will recover)**. God was challenging me to be a vessel of His glory. I also came to understand that as we share with others what God has done in our lives, their faith is increased, and God's anointing (presence) is released. It is up to us to be sensitive to God's Spirit and be available not only to share, but to pray. It is not up to us if anything happens. It is up to God.

The more obedient I was to the Holy Spirit's prompting, the more His power was released during ministry. The Lord also began to release words of knowledge into people's lives, and He encouraged me to start praying for my patients preoperatively. Those prayers brought peace, surgery would go faster, and my patients recovered more quickly. Residents would comment on how well our patients did postoperative.

The Holy Spirit began to teach me how to recognize His voice and to pray believing. One weekend I was home watching our girls when one started to have an asthmatic attack. After I went for her inhaler for the third time, I prayed, and the attack stopped. Several days after praying for her, I was working in the clinic and had a Lutheran theology student's wife as a patient. She was approximately six weeks pregnant and was spotting. The hormone tests indicated that she was going to have a miscarriage. I felt the nudge of the Holy Spirit to pray for her and asked if she believed in healing. She replied that it had ceased after the disciples and apostles died (the same response I would have given before I was healed). I then shared what God had done for me and asked again if I could pray for the pregnancy. She agreed, and as we prayed the presence of God filled the examination room. Her hormone values returned to normal, and she eventually delivered a healthy baby. This experience changed the ministry of her husband. He came to know the Holy Spirit in a new way. He had a living miracle at home.

Another significant event happened during one of our trips to Melodyland. We attended a Thursday morning healing service where a lady was brought forward for prayer by a friend. The friend shared that the lady suffered from depression and had been prayed for by a witch. Pastor Wilkerson had everyone leave the platform except for the lady. As soon as he lifted his hand above her head to pray, the woman fell to the platform and slithered across it like a snake. Pastor Wilkerson's associate pastor and several others took the woman to another room for ministry. At the end of the service, she was brought back to the platform looking much younger and had a beautiful smile on her face. At that time, I said to the Lord, "Yes Lord, I now know that the demonic exists, but I want nothing to do with it. Let someone else do it." That was not to be as you will read later.

Our training in the Holy Spirit continued during the next few years while Donna and I traveled with Pastor Wilkerson. As he ministered, God would give me words of knowledge (**1 Corinthians 12:8**) just before Pastor Wilkerson would speak the same word. While I worked with Pastor Wilkerson, Donna and others would walk among the congregation and be drawn to the individuals whom God was ministering to.

Donna: I don't know that I can fully explain how God was training me (we are never out of training), but in those early days He was teaching me to "hear" His voice. He did it by promptings and giving me words of knowledge. God would show me people in the congregation that He wanted to touch and would either have me pray for them there or bring them forward to the front.

Don: The times with Pastor Wilkerson[1] were an amazing and important time in my spiritual growth. He had a keen sense of the convicting power of the Holy Spirit. I remember how we would go into churches with poor praise and worship, and he would get up to preach saying God is going to save so many people. He would proclaim that a certain number of people needed to come forward and accept the Lord Jesus Christ. I would wonder if he missed it as he just stood there thanking the Lord and at times would challenge Christians in the congregation to believe with him. He just would say, "Thank You, Lord," again and again. Sometimes it seemed to take a long time, but knowing that God spoke to him, he would not let go. Eventually, the convicting power of the Holy Spirit would fall, and people would come forward crying, being convicted of their sins and repenting. I have never known anyone who operated in the convicting power of the Holy Spirit as Pastor Wilkerson did. I thought that it was a unique ministry just for him, but one day the Lord asked me to do the same thing. The Lord built my faith by observing other ministers flowing in the ministry of the Holy Spirit and would challenge me to do the same.

My time at the University of Chicago was one of both spiritual and academic growth. I was at the top of my profession and had favor with both God and man (**1 Samuel 2:26**, "Now the boy Samuel was growing in stature and in favor both with the Lord and with men"). I established a section of Reproductive Endocrinology and Infertility in the Department of Obstetrics and Gynecology. The chairman of the department was an oncologist, Dr. Arthur Herbst, who first reported the association of DES (a synthetic estrogen that was used for the treatment of threaten abortion) with vaginal cancer. He was very supportive of me, and I enjoyed the academic environment. I had a research program, established an endocrine lab after hiring a PhD, and started a fellowship in association with the department of medicine. I had a dual appointment in the Department of Internal

Medicine, Endocrinology Section, and wrote a chapter on infertility in a textbook edited by Dr. Herbst. I began praying with my patients before surgery and felt the peace of the Lord in my practice.

Our university was on the forefront of dealing with pituitary tumors, which had menstrual and reproductive ramifications. I worked closely with the neurosurgeons and endocrinologists in joint interdisciplinary clinics established for patients with those problems. I was also involved with the metabolic research unit at the university through my appointment in Internal Medicine. The Department of Obstetrics and Gynecology was a very academic program modeled after Harvard and had long days during the week and half days on Saturday morning when we did our diabetic teaching for the residents. I even operated in surgical suites where some of the pioneers of obstetrics and gynecology had operated.

Since I took the train to work every day except for the weekend, I would leave early in the morning before the children were up and return late in the evening after they were in bed. With the half day at the hospital on Saturday, I really missed my family, which concerned me, but academically I was alive.

One day I was riding the train to work and reading one of the daily papers, the *Chicago Sun Times*. It had an article about an Oklahoma evangelist, Oral Roberts, who had been called to build a university in Tulsa, Oklahoma. Oral felt that the Lord was calling him to start a medical school that would teach the combination of prayer and medicine. He believed not only in the art of medicine but also in the supernatural healing power of God. The newspaper article was not very complimentary about what the evangelist wanted to do. As I was reading the article, I felt the Lord say to me that I was going there.

The next month I went to a national meeting for obstetricians and gynecologists (Ob/Gyn). I met with the new chairman of the Department of Ob/Gyn at Oral Roberts University School, who was a former Baptist medical missionary to Kenya. When I shared with him my possible interest, he shared what the Lord was doing there. The leading of the Lord to Oklahoma became very evident to me. I shared with Donna, and both of us were very excited about the door that the Lord was opening. I eventually went to visit Tulsa and met the dean, the former dean of the medical school at the University of Tennessee. I was very impressed with him and the other faculty members that I met. The university had provisional approval for the medical school and was enrolling medical students to begin the next year. The basic science departments were completed, and they were starting to concentrate on the clinical departments, stressing the combination of prayer and medicine.

Oh, how this combination of prayer and medicine spoke to my heart. My spirit leaped as I felt God was calling me to join this new medical school. When I got home Donna and I prayed about it and felt the Lord was leading us to Tulsa. It was not an easy decision because I had a tenured position at the University of Chicago that the Lord had given me, my children's college education was secured, and I also had a fellowship program and a funded research program of a quarter million dollars. Yet I felt that God was asking me to give it all up to follow Him. **To be willing to give it all up has been a recurrent theme in my walk with God.** (Is there something that the Lord has been asking you to give up?)

I shared with my chairman that I felt God was calling me to Tulsa, Oklahoma. He tried to offer me more money to stay, but I said that that was not it. He said that I had to share my leaving with the faculty because they would not believe it if he told them. I will never forget the day that I did. I told the faculty that I would be leaving to go to a new medical school because I felt God was calling me there. One of the senior members of the department said, "We have lost faculty members to Harvard before, but I don't recall ever losing any to God." That was the beginning of a new adventure with the Lord.

We sold our house in Flossmoor when the market was not moving and bought a house that was under construction in Tulsa. The house was not finished before our move, so Oral Roberts University (ORU) allowed our family to live in graduate housing until it was.

CHAPTER 3

Oral Roberts
University (ORU)

Mark 16:17,18 These signs will accompany those who have believed: in My name they will cast out demons, they will speak with new tongues; they will pick up serpents, and if they drink any deadly poison, it will not hurt them; they will lay hands on the sick, and they will recover.

It was an exciting but challenging time for me at ORU. I had left an established university as section chief where I had a great deal of authority and autonomy, and an academic position that I had always desired. I accepted a position at ORU as the second member of the department. After resigning from the University of Chicago and before arriving at ORU, I was asked to accept the position as chairman of the Department of OB/GYN, as the chairman had been asked to step down by a new dean. In the developing school, I found I had little authority and could not even make a long-distance telephone call without approval. Quite a challenge for the tenured professor from the University of Chicago. God was dealing with my pride.

It was an exciting time for me as I helped in establishing the start of the medical school. The students were fantastic, and my colleagues were all servants of the Lord. Since I had a PhD in physiology, I worked closely with my basic science colleagues and was involved in the clinical correlations courses that we were introducing in the second year of the medical school. Also, my physiology and pharmacology background enabled me to become involved with graduate students in the pharmacology department.

I had my clinical practice in the Family Practice Center and saw God doing amazing things as I prayed for patients. One day I remember asking the Lord, "Why could I not do this in Chicago?," and I heard Him say, "You could have." I recognized then that the limitations were within me and not with God.

Oral Roberts would have Partners' Meetings where I saw God move. I heard him preach on seed faith[2] and make appeals. I was skeptical at first thinking it was a marketing tool, but then at one meeting, the Lord spoke to me to give. I then began to understand seed faith and how important it is in our Christian walk—another one of God's principles was planted in my heart. Medical teams were assigned at every Partners' Meeting to evaluate and confirm healings. Donna and I worked one meeting where several partners had strange manifestations in which, for instance, a limb would be paralyzed but not following the anatomical nerve distribution for muscle and sensory function. When that was recognized, we would pray in the Spirit and the Lord would give us words of knowledge concerning the situation. As we gave the word to the individual, if they spoke out forgiveness or acknowledged what the Holy Spirit had spoken, they were set free from the demonic forces and were healed. What a powerful Savior we serve.

P.R.Tredway

Oklahoma professional photo, 1979

At the conclusion of the Partners' Meetings, Oral would have the faculty come forward to form prayer lines through which the partners would pass as the faculty prayed. When they passed by me, some would be "slain in the Spirit" (this had been happening when I would pray for people, just as it did in my mentor, Ralph Wilkerson's, ministry). Unfortunately, this caused a backlog of people in the prayer line, and because of this happening, I had to go see Oral Roberts. This did not happen in his ministry at that time. I shared my testimony of what God had done, how He had led me to ORU, and that I was committed to the school.

Oral was very gracious, but I felt a certain reservation from him. I later found out that he had been hurt in the past by others trying to launch their ministry from ORU by riding on his coat tails. I also found out that Oral and Ralph Wilkerson were good friends and that Oral had asked him about me. I would later spend a precious time with Oral and Pastor Wilkerson at Melodyland in California.

Shortly after arriving at ORU, the dean who hired me was fired and a search began for a new dean. The provost, Dr. Jim Winslow, assumed the role of interim dean, and the chairman of Family Practice was appointed the new dean. A struggle began between the two of us because he liked to micromanage.

It was a very difficult time for me because the dean wanted the department of Ob/Gyn to support Family Practice and not to have a training program outside of Family Practice. That was not what the Lord had spoken to me. It was also contrary to the agreement that I had with the original dean who hired me. This resulted in tremendous conflicts between the dean and me. Some of the other basic science chairmen came to me and suggested that I should be dean. While I felt God might be calling me to do that, I waited on the Lord and did not share with anyone. I felt I had to honor the one in authority over me and if there was to be a change, God would remove him. Just as David did not take the opportunity to remove Saul in 1 Samuel 24, I would have no part of any academic removal tactic.

My clinical office was in the Family Practice Center, where I developed many lifetime friendships, especially with Dr. John Crouch. Dr. John Crouch joined the OB/GYN department with me and was a treasure from the Lord in those early days. We had time to pray together and saw God do many wonderful things. He and his family became very close friends. God was good and provided other close relationships to encourage us. Carol Kory, a librarian at ORU, would become part of our extended family and an important prayer warrior for our ministry.

God revealed Himself during this difficult time with the dean. I began to see God do supernatural healings as I prayed for patients. One patient in her late twenties came to see me for secondary amenorrhea (she had only had one menses in her life). After the exam and ordering laboratory tests, I kept seeing a tricycle in my mind. It just would not go away. I eventually said, "I don't understand this, but I keep seeing a tricycle in my mind." She began to cry and shared that as a child there was a great hurt that centered around a tricycle. We prayed about the situation and asked the Lord to heal the emotional hurt. The next day she had a menstrual period.

Another couple came to me because the wife could not get pregnant. I examined her and discovered that she had fibroid tumors of the uterus that resulted in the uterus being the size of a twenty-week pregnancy. The distortion of the uterine cavity affected her ability to become pregnant. They were Christians, and we agreed in prayer for healing of the uterus. There was a young anesthesiologist member of the OB/GYN faculty in the exam room with me. When we prayed, the power of God touched him, and he was slain in the Spirit (Appendix E). The couple and my colleague were excited, for the Spirit of the Lord was in the room. The word then came to me that the couple was to daily lay hands on the area and pray together to curse the tumors. We agreed that they would return in a few weeks for a follow-up.

When they returned (my anesthesiologist friend was there also) the uterus had decreased in size. For the next few months, the uterus decreased to about that of a ten- to twelve-week pregnancy. A later exam revealed that the size of the uterus had increased, and the couple confessed that they had stopped praying. The decision was then made to do the surgery to remove the fibroids. The blood loss was minimal, and the surgery was short. What an exciting time as I began to see the power of prayer in combination with medicine. It is interesting to note that the couple was having marital difficulties when they first came to see me, but the Lord healed their relationship as they prayed together daily.

Pastor Wilkerson invited Donna and me to go with him and his wife to a Full Gospel Businessmen International (FGBMI) meeting in New Orleans. He was to be one of the major speakers, and I was to give my testimony. There was a very large crowd, too large for the auditorium, and it resulted in an overflow of approximately 100-150 people that gathered in another meeting room. Just before the session was to begin, Pastor Wilkerson turned to me and said, "This is what the Lord wants us to do. I will minister in the main auditorium. You will go to the other room and minister." I couldn't believe what was happening. I had never ministered in a group of that size. I opened the meeting with prayer, gave my testimony, and then asked all who wanted prayer to come forward. Most of the people came forward. The presence of God filled the room, and I didn't even have to lay hands on them. Before I approached those who came forward, God touched them, and they were slain in the Spirit.

One morning after returning from the FGBMI meeting, the Lord spoke to me as I was running on the track at the ORU aerobic center. He told me to go to Los Angeles the following weekend. I then felt impressed to call the associate pastor of Melodyland, Cecil Pumphrey, to share what the Lord had said. Cecil immediately planned for me to speak at several Bible studies—one on Friday night after my arrival and two on Saturday. There was a wonderful move of God at the Bible studies and a precious time for me to experience His guidance and anointing. Eventually, Pastor Wilkerson invited me to have a monthly Sunday evening healing service at Melodyland. Once a month for a year I would fly to Los Angeles to do the service and would take the Sunday night "red eye" back to Tulsa in time to go to work at ORU.

My time at ORU was a precious time of growing in God. I learned something from Oral Roberts that changed my life. In one of his teachings on praying in the Holy Spirit[3] (tongues), he said to quiet your mind after praying and listen, and that God would speak to you in your mind. This opened a new communication with the heavenly Father. I learned that if at times I did not have a word of knowledge for the person I was praying for, I could pray in the Spirit and God would speak to me as I listened. If I didn't hear anything, I knew that I was still praying a perfect prayer. I will be forever grateful for the input that Oral Roberts[4] and Ralph Wilkerson[1] have had on my life.

During one of the monthly healing services at Melodyland, a man came forward for healing of an elbow that had been injured. He was unable to straighten his arm. As I prayed, the Spirit of the Lord came upon him, and he was slain in the Spirit. When he got up his arm was the same but there was no doubt that God had touched him. That puzzled me. A few weeks later this man stopped by my office in Tulsa. As he walked into my office, I could see that his elbow was healed. He related that after the meeting in California, the Lord had convicted him of some bitterness that he had in his heart toward a former friend who had offended him. He was returning from Arkansas where he had gone to ask for forgiveness from that individual. As he did what the Lord had convicted him to do, he was healed. God began to show me another way He heals through inner healing and forgiveness (Appendix B).

In February 1979, Donna and I attended the annual meeting of the American Fertility Society in San Francisco where I spoke in one of the seminars. (We were still living in Tulsa at that time.) When the convention was over, we visited friends who lived in the area. They knew us when I was disabled, saw the results of God's healing, and were excited to visit and to hear of the things God was doing in our lives. They at one time lived with us when they lost their house to a mudslide. The husband had recently lost his job, their two young boys were being treated for a bleeding disorder (hemophilia), the wife had had a stroke and was paralyzed on one side, was blind in one eye, and was also being treated for a blood disorder. Both she and the boys were being treated for rheumatoid arthritis. While at the medical meeting, the couple notified us that they had separated but together were wanting to meet us. We met them in their home and shared things we had done and learned. While talking to them, one of the things we shared was the story of the woman at Melodyland who had been prayed for by a witch. Our lady friend started to laugh and the atmosphere in the room changed. Her husband and I excused ourselves, and I went to the restroom.

Donna: When the men were out of the room, I said to her that the story wasn't a laughing matter and that things like that really do happen. She then said, "I am not laughing. I have been prayed for by a witch and so have my sons, but don't tell my husband. He'll get mad." Her mother had taken her and her sons to a lady to be prayed for. Her mother also took our friend's bed sheets and night clothing to the lady to pray over them during the time of her illness. I could not keep that to myself, so when the men returned, I knew that I had to say something. My friend was right. Her husband got mad. At that point, Don decided that we needed to go, and he suggested that we pray together before we left. We gathered in a circle, and Don started. I was holding my friend's hand, and suddenly she flopped to the floor and started to manifest. I tried to get Don's attention, but his eyes were closed tight, and he would not respond to anything I did to try to get his attention. I usually pray with my eyes open so was very aware of what was happening. Finally Don opened his eyes. This was our first encounter with a demonic presence. I ran to the phone and asked several people to pray for us, and Don started taking authority over it.

Don: An anger rose in me when I saw what was happening to my Christian friend. We prayed for deliverance in the name of Jesus, and He began to set her free. I never will forget what happened when she opened her blind eye. She saw my necktie and commented on how beautiful it was. Her arm and leg became stronger but not completely healed. We also prayed for her children, who had been prayed for by the same witch. They were healed of their blood disorder and arthritis. We were leaving the next morning for Tulsa, so we called our friends who lived in the area and asked them to come and to continue ministry. Pastor Cecil Pumphrey from Melodyland was also contacted and asked to come. He flew to San Francisco the next day. The three of them ministered to our friend for approximately a week and took her through multiple sessions of deliverance. By the week's end, all functions returned, and our friend was totally healed. Her healing was confirmed by her physician and therapists when she returned for an evaluation.

Our friend shared her testimony in church a few days later. She said that she could not hear me when I started sharing about the lady who was delivered at Melodyland and heard loud screams in her head before falling to the floor when we started to pray. She shared about the warmth she experienced in her head and seeing the most beautiful tie she had ever seen when she opened her blind eye. What a Savior we have.

God taught me an important lesson through that deliverance experience. The ministry of Jesus for today includes deliverance, just as it did in the past. We are to minister no differently than the disciples or the seventy-two whom Jesus sent out (Appendix B and D).

Mark 16:15-18 And He said to them, "Go into all the world and preach the gospel to all creation. He who has believed and has been baptized shall be saved; but he who has disbelieved shall be condemned. These signs will accompany those who have believed: in My name they will cast out demons, they will speak with new tongues; they will pick up serpents, and if they drink any deadly poison, it will not hurt them; they will lay hands on the sick, and they will recover."

One day at Melodyland, a lady in the audience came to me after I spoke and asked to pray for me. I allowed her to and felt nothing when she prayed. The lady looked at me very strangely. An associate pastor came to me and said, "I am amazed at your courage." I didn't understand what he meant by that, and he went on to explain that she was a witch. For a few weeks after that, especially at night when I was tired, her face would appear in my mind. I would rebuke her in Jesus' name, and after two or three incidences, it stopped happening. I sensed that she was trying to come against me and to probably curse me. The anointing of God protected me, but I also learned to be careful when receiving prayer.

One weekend when I was at Melodyland, Pastor Pumphrey introduced me to Loren Cunningham,[5] the founder of Youth With A Mission (YWAM). He and his wife, Darlene, were hosting an evening program on the Trinity Broadcasting Network (TBN) in Orange County, California. YWAM leaders from different parts of the world shared, and it was exciting to hear what God was doing throughout the world. The significance of this meeting will become apparent later.

Dr. John Coppes and I traveled with Pastor Pumphrey and a group from Melodyland to Mexico City. The meetings were arranged by a local missionary, Wayne Myers of Christ for the Nations. What a privilege it was to spend time with such a man of faith. One evening as I was speaking at a meeting, the glory of God filled the room and several people started to manifest as the presence of God drove the enemy to the surface. What a time in the Lord we had as God set His people free.

Ralph Wilkerson called while I was in Mexico City and asked me to return to Melodyland to minister in the following Sunday night service. That Sunday night service was profound. The Spirit of the Lord fell with conviction on the congregation. A man spontaneously came forward with tears streaming down his face seeking Jesus as his Savior. God then continued to move throughout the congregation with healings, fillings of the Holy Spirit, and salvations. What a glorious night it was! Pastor Wilkerson wanted me to stay and said that if I wanted, he would call Oral so that I could stay to help continue the move of God. He felt that it was the beginning of a revival. I declined, afraid to have him call Oral, for I felt I needed to return to my practice at ORU. I still had difficulty balancing medical practice and public ministry. I often wonder what would have happened if I had accepted that challenge. I believe that I missed God that day.

Donna and I also had multiple opportunities to share at home groups in Tulsa. One evening we spoke at a small Chinese gathering. There was a man there with a leg several inches shorter than the other who had to wear a shoe with a lift. He was prayed for, and the leg grew out to match the other. The group was so excited as the presence of the Lord filled the room.

Tulsa seemed to be the buckle of the Bible belt in the late 70s and early 80s. We were blessed to be exposed to such ministries as Kenneth Hagin, John Osteen, Kenneth Copeland, T.L. Osborn, and others. Our family became members of Grace Fellowship in Tulsa in 1979 and sat under the teaching ministry of Pastors Ken Stewart and Bob Yandian. Our daughters attended Grace school, and we had a church group that met monthly in our home. I will be eternally grateful for all the men and women of God He has sent across our path. I am especially grateful for the ministry and teaching of Bob Yandian,[6] who instilled in me a love for the Word of God. What an inspiration and challenge he has been in my life. An important principle of the Lord I learned is to observe how the Holy Spirit moves in others and to glean from it what the Lord has for you. **Sometimes it will take an anointing of God to spark an anointing in another's life.**

We developed lifelong relationships with many of those in our monthly home church group. Together there was spiritual growth, healings, deliverances, and much more. We even experienced God multiplying a pot of stew when there was no way that we had enough to feed the group.

In addition to our home group, Donna and I had opportunities to share in other small groups and in congregations. One evening I shared my testimony with a Chinese home group of twenty to thirty people. We had a prayer time, and a man asked for prayer for his back pain. I had a word about a short leg, and we prayed for the lengthening of one of his legs. Donna has a special anointing for this, so as she joined me in prayer, the Lord dramatically lengthened his leg. The group became so excited, and we saw faith arise in a very powerful way. Again, God confirmed His Word with signs and wonders. This was the beginning of my ministry to Asia. I have always felt more at ease in Asia than any other part of the world.

The enemy looks for opportunities to discourage moving in God's anointing. We would be attacked especially in the home after times of ministry. Our children would become unruly, a toilet would be plugged, and equipment wouldn't work. He even attacked physically. One night as I was sleeping, I awoke choking with what seemed like a hand on my throat. I couldn't speak out, but Donna woke up, sensed what was happening, and commanded it to let go in the name of Jesus. The presence left.

There were multiple spiritual battles as we moved forward in ministry and wondered if there might be an "open door" that was allowing the enemy to attack. One day as Donna was looking into the dining room, a dining room chair stood out and appeared very large. God showed her that the back of the chair was in the shape of a Shinto Tori gate. When I was in the Navy stationed in Japan, I bought a beautiful teak wood dining room table for twelve, complete with twelve "Tori Gate" backed chairs and a matching hutch. There was also a beautiful cherry wood coffee table and end tables that had hand-carved Tori Gate scenes. I had also bought a hope chest that had decorative dragons on brass straps going around the chest. The Lord told us to burn them all. We did. In addition, my father had been a Shriner in freemasonry and my mother had given me all his regalia. God had us burn that also. Many of the items would not burn easily until we pleaded the blood of Jesus Christ over them and asked for forgiveness for bringing those items into our home even though it was done out of ignorance. With that, they were rapidly consumed in the fire, sometimes almost in a flash.

Through that experience, we began to see how the enemy tries to ensnare people, even in their innocence, by surrounding themselves with items that are an abomination to the Lord. We have also seen Christians brought into bondage by surrounding themselves with items that were dedicated to the devil. God says in **Hosea 4:6** My people are destroyed for a lack of knowledge.

God began to teach me more about His character during our time in Tulsa. He used our third oldest daughter, Kimberly, to demonstrate His compassionate love for His children. She was a very hyper child. One weekend she had a friend spend the night who was equally hyper. I must say, I was glad when they went to bed. My study was next to Kimberly's bedroom, and as was my custom before going to bed, I looked in on the girls. I noted how peaceful Kimberly and her friend looked as they slept. I overlooked their rambunctious behavior and felt compassion toward them. The Lord spoke to my heart and said that that is the way He sees me. He overlooks my "rambunctious" behavior and accepts me with His compassionate love.

I had another revelation from God a few weeks later using the same scenario. Kimberly and her friend were peacefully sleeping when I checked in on them. While I enjoyed her friend, my attraction to Kimberly was greater because she was the offspring of my blood. God said, "That's how I see you." As I was standing there pondering what the Lord had said, Kimberly started to stir. She woke up startled and was full of fear. She started to look around in the dark room, but when she saw me, her father, her face changed from fear to one of recognition and relief. She smiled and lifted her arms up to me. **What a joyful feeling it was. God spoke to me and said that He too is joyful when I recognize Him as Father and hold up my arms for His security and comfort.** How often when we are fearful do we forget that He is there. I believe that that recognition of who the Father is, is true worship, and it greatly pleases Him.

More growth in the Lord and more challenges came during my time at ORU. The faculty was challenging the students to go to the mission field. One day the Lord spoke to me and asked, "Are you willing to do what you are asking your students to do?" Our friend from Melodyland, Pastor Cecil Pumphrey, had gone to Youth With A Mission (YWAM) to do a Discipleship Training School (DTS) in Kona, Hawaii. The school consisted of three months of lectures focused on the character of God and covered topics such as how to hear God's voice, what is His call on your life, intercession, and spiritual warfare. After the lecture phase, there was a two and a half month outreach where the class was to apply what they learned.

Cecil and I had become close friends during our time at Melodyland, and he was someone whom I had great respect for. He would give away 80 to 90 percent of his earnings, and I saw how the Lord blessed him. His letters from Hawaii about the lecture phase, and those from Hong Kong describing the team's outreach to Viet Nam refugees, stirred my spirit. While in Hong Kong, the YWAM team went into the camps and shoveled out human refuse around broken toilets and then repaired the toilets. Other volunteer agencies had refused to do it. Because of that work, YWAM gained favor with the Hong Kong government and was given freedom in the camps and to also establish a YWAM base on Hong Kong Island. I wanted to find out more information about YWAM (this was before the Internet), but I could not find any. It is interesting how God orchestrates our walk with Him without us knowing it. Recall, I had met Loren Cunningham, the founder of Youth With A Mission, earlier in the Los Angeles area at TBN. He was to become another servant of God who has had a major impact on my life. His book, *Is That Really You, God?*,[5] was an inspiration to me.

It seems that with every call of God, there are struggles that attempt to block that call. How we handle those struggles determine how we grow in the understanding of God's character. One of the ways that the enemy used against me was the difficult situation with the dean and struggling not to become bitter and resentful. God gave me two precious friends, Robert Hermann, who was chairman of the Biochemistry Department, and Jimmie Valentine, a pharmacology professor, who helped me grow in God and not in bitterness. The Lord was also dealing with another wrong attitude, pride.

The situation at ORU became more difficult, and I began to pray about whether God was calling us to YWAM. One week I had two different patients from YWAM. I had never had patients from there before. Cecil had also shared that YWAM had a mercy ship called the *Anastasis*. With my Navy and medical background, that really spoke to me, and we began to feel that the Lord was calling us to do a DTS in Kona and then to go to the *Anastasis*. I had had a word of the Lord about establishing the Obstetrics and Gynecology Department at ORU, but my timing was off. The fulfillment was to come later.

Following the anointing of God requires you to guard your heart. There will be sufferings as well as testings, and dealings of wrong attitudes that need correcting. Looking back, I can see how the Lord used my difficult relationship with the dean to grow in Him. God was certainly dealing with the pride of life in me.

> **Philippians 3:10** that I may know Him and the power of His resurrection and the fellowship of His sufferings, being conformed to His death.

> **Philippians 3:14,15** I press on toward the goal for the prize of the upward call of God in Christ Jesus. Let us therefore, as many as are perfect, have this attitude; and if in anything you have a different attitude, God will reveal that also to you.

These two scriptures have become the walk of my life with God in the understanding of His character. One must learn to walk in forgiveness and humility.

With all the exciting things of God happening in my life and practice, my relationship with the dean deteriorated to the point that my professional life was very difficult. I would be called to have multiple meetings with him and would have to wait a couple of hours. Nothing I did pleased him. Both Bob Herman and I were on his bad list, and it became so bad that the provost of the university called the three of us into his office to try to make peace. Bob and I tried but to no avail.

One Sunday while I was still at ORU, I shared my testimony at a local church, and the Lord again confirmed His Word with healings. He was teaching me how to combine medicine and prayer. It was so exciting to know that I was in the place where God wanted me despite the difficulties. I also learned another important lesson, that when God moves, the enemy will try to steal your victory. I don't remember what happened, but Donna and I got into a silly argument that night. I went to work Monday morning with a troubled heart—what a mood swing in twenty-four hours.

As I was walking across the ORU campus, I developed a rapid pulse rate with chest pain. I felt cold and clammy and went to see the chairman of the Department of Family Medicine. I had EKG changes, and the next thing I knew I was in an ambulance on my way to St. John's Hospital Cardiac Care Unit just twenty-four hours after being used of God in a healing service. I was 38 years old. In the ambulance I remembered my 52-year-old father dying in my arms of a heart attack. In addition, two uncles had died at an early age with a heart attack, and my grandfather had had multiple heart attacks. I was filled with fear. I wanted to pray, but I was in pain and so fearful that I couldn't. They sedated and monitored me and planned to do a cardiac catheterization in the morning. Donna told me later that a pastor friend came that evening and prayed against a spirit of death. (At that time, I had no understanding of what that meant.) The doctor had also told her that I would probably not survive if I had another episode of chest pain.

The next morning, I was taken to the cath lab for an angiogram. I later learned that at that exact time, the faculty of the Anatomy Department at ORU was meeting for prayer and were praying for me. One professor had a vision of a blocked coronary artery that was being opened by the power of God. My arteriogram was normal. I still remember my cardiologist telling me that the results did not match the EKG or clinical findings. Once again, I battled against infirmary. It has become a recurrent theme for me during my life. Through pain and suffering I have come to know the Lord in a very special and tangible way. God delivered me from the chest pain, and I understood another scripture.

> 2 Timothy 2:13 If we are faithless, He remains faithful, for He cannot deny Himself.

As I had my battles following God's anointing, Donna had her own. God brought someone into our lives for her. One Sunday morning before the girls and Donna arrived in Tulsa, I was on the ORU campus before going to church and saw a young man sitting in a car in the parking lot. I felt the Holy Spirit telling me to go to him. I did and asked if I could be of some help. He told me his name, that he was from California and was looking for the Sunday service at ORU. I told him that the students, staff, and faculty went to local churches and invited him to go to church with me. We spent the day together fellowshipping, and the Lord had me share my walk with Him as to why I had come to ORU. He then shared that he was from the Los Angeles area, had developed one of the first mobile phone systems in LA, and was wanting to go deeper in God. Later that afternoon he left to return to the West Coast. It was an encounter that I knew the Lord set up but for what purpose, I did not know. Almost a year later, I received a call from him saying that he was back in town and wanted to see us. I will let Donna tell the rest of the story.

Donna: The enemy can be very subtle and patient when moving to bring about destruction in a person's life. He attempts to lay negative platforms that he can build upon in insidious ways. As I look back there is no situation that I can pinpoint to say that this is where it all started except to say that we were having difficulties in our marriage. I felt rejected, misunderstood, not believed, or trusted with the things that God had showed me. I grew to not like myself and felt that if I didn't like me, how could God? I let myself go, so to speak, in not necessarily keeping up with my appearance and didn't think that it mattered to anyone anyway.

I can't recall how it came about, but a young man came to visit us in our home. He obviously knew my state of mind, and one day when Don was at work and the girls were in school, he told me to put on a dress instead of jeans and to put on make-up. I fought him and said no. I don't recall what he said or how he persuaded me, but I did. We went for a ride and lunch, and all the while he talked and encouraged me into who I really was. It was a very difficult and emotional time as I had a hard time believing what he said. The next day he told me to make an appointment to get my hair done. I fought, cried, and said no. I lost again and made the appointment.

When we returned home, he said, "Now I want you to put on some nice clothes and go meet your husband when he gets home." I said no because I felt that Don would make fun of me. I told the young man that the first thing Don would say when he saw me would be, "What did you do to your hair?" I just wanted to get out of my nice clothes, put on my jeans, and soak my head. The young man literally grabbed me and took me to my bathroom mirror and made me look at myself. I struggled and tried not to look, but he made me and told me how nice I looked.

When Don came home that evening, I was made to meet him with my nice clothes and fixed hair. As soon as he came in the door, he took one look at me and said, "What did you do to your hair?" I was crushed. I burst into tears, ran up the stairs, and headed to the bathroom to soak my head and to change my clothes. The young man stopped me. Again, I don't remember what he said, but whatever it was, it kept me from doing what I set out to do. Instead, I went to the bathroom mirror and liked what I saw and decided that I didn't care what anyone else thought. I was going to look nice for me. That was the turning point in my life where I began to like myself again.

I am not sure when I gained the understanding of God's love for me. It might have been during the time mentioned above or later in YWAM, but I feel led to share it here. It came by seeing a straight horizontal line like this: GOD _____. I have always been told that God is love and that His love never changes. It is constant and there is nothing one can do to change it. Through that straight line I received the revelation that no matter how many times I've messed up or how much work I did for Him, that line could not be moved. I could not make Him love me less, or more, no matter what I did. His love is constantly the same. He never changes. Through that I also learned that I have never been rejected; by mankind, yes, but not by the One that was there at my conception. That is where my acceptance and identity lay. It is what God thinks of me, not mankind.

Don: Dr. Betsy Neuenschwander, a young female obstetrician/gynecologist who was in practice in Tennessee, contacted me in late winter of 1980. She had a precious spirit, loved the Lord, and believed God was calling her to ORU. It was evident that God had His hand on her, and with a witness of the Spirit, I offered her an assistant Professor position. Both she and her husband, Mark, felt called to the mission field. Mark had completed a residency in Family Practice, was also interested in surgery, and started a fellowship in General Surgery with Dr. D.L. Moore. Mark and Betsy were in Tulsa for nine months initially between June 1980—March 1981. They left ORU in 1981 to go to Chicago, where Betsy took a second residency in Family Practice and Mark completed his surgery training. They returned to the City of Faith in June 1984 and played an important part in ministry there and later launched into a profound ministry overseas. I saw in them a great passion and zeal for the Lord. They were, and still are, a blessing. They will never know how much they ministered to me as I battled with the dean. While they were still at ORU, I left for YWAM.

The year before leaving for YWAM, the Lord had me give away all our savings. We only had enough funds for the first six months. I tried to sell my house, but it would not sell. At the last minute a group of six students from Rhema Bible School believed the Lord was directing them to live in our house and pay the mortgage and utilities. One even took over the payments of my pride and joy, a Mercedes car. Again, I saw the faithfulness of the Lord when stepping out in faith. We shipped our family Plymouth van to Hawaii and were commissioned and sent forth from Grace Fellowship as missionaries with monthly support.

I never will forget, as Pastor Bob Yandian was praying for me in that church service, he and I were both slain in the Spirit. A prophetic word was given during that service that I was anointed and sent forth in the order of Melchizedek **(Genesis 14:18)**, confirming the previous prophecy of Ralph Wilkerson. I had no understanding at that time what that meant as I was still learning what it meant to follow God's anointing (Holy Spirit).

The dean was pleased that I was leaving. There was a faculty dinner shortly after I shared with him that I believed God was leading me to YWAM. At the dinner the new chairman, a private obstetrician/gynecologist friend of mine from the community, was introduced. I, as well as others in the room, was surprised as I was not aware that he had been hired. The way the process was handled was quite an embarrassment for me. God had to deal with me regarding bitterness toward the dean.

My academic contract with ORU finished at the end of July 1980. We did not have to be in Hawaii until September. Our four daughters stayed with my mother and stepfather in southern Illinois while Donna and I had some church and FGBMFI meetings in Alabama, Mississippi, and Southern California.

What powerful times we had in God as He confirmed we were in His will by leaving for Youth With a Mission Many lives were touched by His Spirit. I recall one FGBMFI meeting in Birmingham, Alabama, when I sensed during the preliminaries that the Lord wanted to minister even before I spoke. I interrupted the program and said that God wanted to move, and immediately His Spirit filled the auditorium. I will never forget what happened next. A woman in a wheelchair, paralyzed from the waist down due to an auto accident, got up and walked unattended by the power of God. Multiple people came forward and were touched by the Lord. Praise and worship continued until the morning hours as God blessed His people. The leadership later wanted to take up an offering, and the Lord told me to write a check for one thousand dollars. I could not believe that He asked me to do that as I needed the money to help support us for the next four months. The next morning, I was sitting at breakfast at the hotel where we were staying, and a man who I had never seen before came and gave me a check for $1000 dollars. He said the Lord told him to bring me the check. A few weeks later the Lord had me give another $1000 donation, and again the Lord had someone I did not know bring me a check for $1000 within twenty-four hours. God was confirming His will, and I was learning to listen to His voice.

We picked up the children from my parents in Illinois, drove our RV to Los Angeles, and attended the annual August Charismatic Clinic in Melodyland before going to Hawaii. I had a teaching session during the clinic, and the Lord had me speak on fear. He used my experience with the heart, and to explain fear from a physiological and spiritual basis. It was a powerful time of ministry as the Lord set people free. The Lord spoke to me that if I based the battles in my life upon His Word, He would release tremendous power confirming the word that Pastor Wilkerson gave me.

During our time at Melodyland, one of the evening speakers was Jack Hayford, senior pastor of Church on the Way in Van Nuys, California, who spoke on worship. He was a very humble man who told his story about God's presence coming into his church. His non-assuming way had an impact on my life. He was also a songwriter and had written the worship song "Majesty." That evening he introduced worship in a very special way, and the congregation of over a thousand people were on their knees worshiping God. It was a profound experience. I had the opportunity to hear him on multiple occasions and have been blessed by his walk with God and his insight[7] in the area of worship. A recent biography of Pastor Hayford has been published which I highly recommend.[8]

After several exciting months of knowing that we were in the will of God, it was time to go to Hawaii and YWAM. While we were waiting in the Los Angeles airport to leave for Kona, our name was called over the intercom. Our whole family was upgraded to first class on a 747 flight to Honolulu. Oh how the girls enjoyed the flight in the upper deck. Donna and I rejoiced at the faithfulness of God. We had no doubt that the Lord was leading.

CHAPTER 4

YWAM DTS
Kona, *Hawaii*

John 14:7 If you had known Me, you would have known My Father also; from now on you know Him and have seen Him.

I never will forget the eyes of Peter Jordan, our DTS leader, when he picked us up at the Kona airport. He was shocked when he saw all the luggage. Donna and I plus our four daughters (ages 13, 11, 9 and 7) had matching luggage, two bags and a handbag each. We filled the pickup. (He often told the story of our arrival and the number of bags.) We were taken to our small two-bedroom and one-bath apartment, which was a tight quarter for us, especially when each girl was accustomed to her own room. My big hurdle was sharing the one bathroom with Donna and the four girls. I had to get up early in the morning if I wanted to use it. It was an exciting and challenging life for us as we followed God.

While Donna and I went to class, the girls attended a missionary school for the children of staff and students. The DTS was a wonderful time for Donna and me. I finally could take time off from medicine to better hear the voice of the Lord. We had wonderful staff and speakers, and we soaked up the teaching. We learned about the character of God, hearing God's voice, spiritual warfare, and what His call was on our lives. I enjoyed spending time with the family and in the Word since medicine had occupied so much of my life.

There was a millipede infestation on the island at that time that I identified to a certain extent with the plagues of Egypt. We would shovel them up in the streets and walkways in the mornings and fought them in the apartment. If you rolled on them at night, they would leave an acid stain on your skin. One morning our youngest woke up with a ring on her face from one. It was almost too much for me.

All students had two hours of work duty on weekday afternoons, and mine was that of the base doctor. I had obtained a Hawaiian medical license before going to Hawaii, so my work duty became that of the base doctor. We had one very small simple room with a flat exam table and desk for a clinic. My nurse was a Norwegian who had just returned with Dengue fever from the refugee camps of Thailand. The clinic had very little equipment and was quite a change for me after leaving academic medical centers as a sub-specialist and now practicing primary care medicine in a small dark room that was once used for refrigeration.

I had been an author of chapters in textbooks and of scientific articles, but now I had to look things up again in the medical reference books I had brought.

I never will forget the day when a few-weeks-old infant was brought in with a fever. I asked the nurse for the thermometer, but it had been broken a few weeks before. That just about did it for me.

As I left the clinic that afternoon, I had a very frank conversation with God saying, "God, someone is going to die here, and it is going to be Your fault!" I will always remember what the Lord then spoke to my mind. He asked, "What are you going to do about it?" That statement got through my thick skull. I then went out and bought a thermometer and other medical supplies that night. The next day some donations came to the clinic. I learned an important principle of God. **He had put me there, and it should end up being a better place when I left than when I came.**

Sometimes one may tend to think that he is the only one who has sacrificed leaving home to follow God. Our class was around forty to fifty students, and all had felt the call of God to come to the DTS. I recall one man who had left his job with only a few months before retirement. He sacrificed the security of a retirement income to follow the call of God. Of course, we were there just like everyone else walking out in faith what God had for us. I also learned an important principle: **You cannot teach faith unless you walk it yourself.**

The teachers were wonderful and were from all around the world. Two had a profound effect on my life. Campbell McAlpine from the UK, who was a tremendous Bible teacher, and Jack Winter of Daystar Ministries in the US, who taught on the Father-heart of God[9] and how the image of our earthly father affects our image of God the Father. I had a good dad, but he was of English heritage and not overly affectionate. As Jack was speaking and praying for our class, the Lord showed me that I always had wanted to be held on my father's lap but never was. As Jack prayed for me during a time of ministry, the Lord held me on His lap. **That day God began to show me how He wants to make up for deficiencies in our lives.** I will have more to say about the Father-heart of God in a future chapter. Jack became a friend and fellowshipped with us in our home in Kona when he taught at the Kona YWAM base.

There was another day during Jack's ministry that I saw God do a very deep healing. One of our female students was in Kona accompanied by her younger teenage brother. The Lord was moving in inner healing as Jack Winters taught on misconceptions of God that were the result of issues with our parents. Our class was held in an open pavilion, and this young lady openly shared that she could never trust God because her father had sexually abused her since she was a young girl. The abuse eventually resulted in a pregnancy. Her brother was her son. As she forgave her father, she broke, cried, and the Lord ministered to her. At the time that she was openly sharing, unnoticed by her and the class, her brother (son) had been watching and listening to her confession. I never will forget how he walked forward to her in front of the class saying out loud that he had always wanted her to be his mom. There was not a dry eye in the class that day. How God must look down on us and want us to be made whole. Praise You, Father, for Your loving-kindness.

> Psalm 17:7 Wondrously show Your lovingkindness, O Savior of those who take refuge at Your right hand....

Many emotional healings took place during the DTS, and the class became a very close-knit family. We became close not only with our fellow students but also with the staff. Donna and Peter Jordan were the leaders along with Dean and Michelle Sherman, Dr. Bruce and Barbara Thompson, David Ross (from Korea), and the Scratches (Darlene Cunningham's parents). All would have major impacts on our lives and become lifelong friends and fellow workers in the kingdom. Our DTS was also in the early days of YWAM's establishing the Pacific and Asia University (later to become University of the Nations), and we were privileged to meet Howard Malmstadt, PhD, the co-founder along with Loren Cunningham. We would join Dr. Bruce Thompson in the early days of the College of Counseling and Health Care after our DTS.

Another teacher was Noel Gibson, accompanied by his wife, Phyl, from Australia. He was a former open-air campaigner from New Zealand and had a powerful ministry from years of experience with that organization. He and his wife were used mightily in inner healing[10] and deliverance.[11] We shared our ministry experiences of the power of God with them and witnessed Noel be released in God's power in a very special way after Donna and I prayed for him. (He had never had people slain in the Spirit when he prayed for them.) The next day after our time together, Noel, with arms raised and eyes closed tight, began to pray for a student. The student fell under the power of God as Noel continued to pray with his eyes shut and arms raised. It was priceless to see his reaction when he stopped praying, opened his eyes, and saw the student on the floor. It was wonderful to see a mighty servant of the Lord realize that the Lord still had more for him after so many years of service. What a lesson, **God is never finished with us as we continue in our Christian walk.**

Philippians 1:6 For I am confident of this very thing, that He who began a good work in you will perfect it until the day of Christ Jesus.

Our fellowship and friendship with Noel and Phyl grew over the years. Donna and I will be forever indebted to God for this precious couple and the time we were able to spend with them during our times in Australia. We will talk more about them later.

CHAPTER 5

YWAM Refugee Camps

Luke 10:2 And He was saying to them, "The harvest is plentiful, but the laborers are few; therefore, beseech the Lord of the harvest to send out laborers into His harvest."

YWAM Kona had become involved in mercy ministries not only through the ship *Anastasis* but also through refugee relief in Thailand for the Cambodians, and in Hong Kong for the Vietnamese.

Deuteronomy 15:11 For the poor will never cease to be in the land; therefore, I command you, saying, "You shall freely open your hand to your brother, to your needy and poor in your land."

Psalm 72:13,14 He will have compassion on the poor and needy, And the lives of the needy he will save. He will rescue their life from oppression and violence, and their blood will be precious in his sight.

Toward the end of our three-month lecture phase (in the month of November), the leadership of the base decided to send Dr. Bruce

FOLLOWING THE *Anointing*: PART I

Thompson (one of our staff) for a month to minister to the YWAM teams and bases in Hong Kong and Thailand. They felt that I was to accompany him, and we would join other healthcare workers. I was excited since this was a fulfillment of what the Lord spoke to me as a teenager (called to be a medical missionary). We flew from Hawaii to Hong Kong, where we stayed for a few days.

The YWAM base leader in Hong Kong was Gary Stephens (brother of Don Stephens of Mercy Ministries). Bruce was sharing on "Openness and Brokenness" in multiple meetings as we met with YWAM workers. The message was foreign to me but one that I needed to hear. I am of English heritage and had difficulty sharing my feelings. Also, as a physician, I was taught to be objective and do not get personally involved with patients. After hearing Bruce's talk multiple times, the message finally broke through. God brought Dr. Thompson in my life to do a deep work of the Holy Spirit in my life. The message of facing who you really are is so important in our walk with God. At that time, Bruce was formulating his dynamic teaching regarding "Walls of My Heart." [12] So often we react in the opposite of what we feel on the inside and build up walls to keep others and God away.

From Hong Kong, we went to Bangkok and from there to the refugee camps at Khao-I-Dang, Thailand. We traveled with another UK physician and in Thailand met more YWAM leaders. YWAM workers once again did the tasks that no one else wanted to do and were blessed because of it and were given more responsibility. It was during the monsoon season, and I never will forget having to wade in water up to my knees with all sorts of debris floating by to get to our housing accommodations. Our shower was cold water in a large clay jug from which a dipper was used to pour over our bodies. The jar was next to the slit in the floor that was our toilet.

Our bed was under a mosquito net. One certainly begins to appreciate what we take for granted in our Western lifestyles.

> **James 4:10,** Humble yourselves in the presence of the Lord, and He will exalt you.

As I met people from different ministries in Khao-I-Dang, it seemed there were three categories of individuals: (1) Christians fulfilling ministry to the poor and afflicted; (2) adventurists; and (3) those who themselves were hurting and ministering to people who were worse off than themselves. These categories were not clear-cut, some having combinations of the three.

As a subspecialist in the middle of the Thailand Cambodian refugee camp, the people did not need an infertility expert. They had basic needs that needed to be met, and I found myself once again using my basic medicine skills. A couple of experiences in these camps spoke to me. One day I found myself in a leprosy ward. During my medical training, I had never seen a case of leprosy and consequently felt very inadequate and asked myself what I had to help these patients.

I was introduced to a young lady in her late teens who was disfigured, having lost a good portion of her nose. Like many young ladies, her initial concern was how anyone could love her and whether she would be able to marry and have a family. It broke my heart as she shared. I shared about the love of God with her, and she came to the understanding of the Lord Jesus Christ. As she accepted the Lord, she no longer felt disfigured and knew in her heart that Jesus loved and died for her. What a witness to the love of God. **We are all disfigured in different ways, but He loves us despite our "disfigurement."**

Romans 8:38,39 For I am convinced that neither death, nor life, nor angels, nor principalities, nor things present, nor things to come, nor powers, nor height, nor depth, nor any other created thing, will be able to separate us from the love of God, which is in Christ Jesus our Lord.

There was another encounter that greatly impacted me. It occurred when I met a former banker from Phnom Penh after a Sunday church service. He described how he had seen his wife and children killed. One of his daughters was pregnant, and he had been made to watch as Pol Pot's soldiers bayoneted his daughter's abdomen, cutting out the baby. He was not sure why, but his life was spared, and he was sent to a re-education farm to work as a peasant in the fields. He was able to escape from the camp and ended up in the Khao-I-Dang refugee camp. He shared that Buddha had not helped him or his family, but after he accepted Jesus, he was able to forgive the soldiers. With that act, he had a new peace and a new purpose in life. **What a witness to the power of forgiveness through the cross of Jesus Christ.**

Acts 26:18 to open their eyes so that they may turn from darkness to light and from the dominion of Satan to God, that they may receive forgiveness of sins and an inheritance among those who have been sanctified by faith in Me.

Bruce Thompson: During a tour of the camp, we were also taken into a camp school for younger children. As we entered a class our team became silent. Hung across the classroom were pictures drawn by the children. They had been given some drawing skills and told to draw whatever they liked. Most of the pictures were of the atrocities they had observed by Pol Pot's brutality. One had drawn a picture of people lined up under a guard and at the end of the line was a tree where they were brutalized to death and then carried away. These pictures shocked and stunned us all as we visualized the tragedy and brutality of a genocide.

It was a comfort to know that some of these children were being introduced to the Healer of broken hearts, who sets the captive free and comforts those who mourn—Jesus Himself in fulfillment of **Isaiah 61.**

Khao-I-Dang Refugee Camp, Thailand, 1980

Don: The Lord did something in my heart in the refugee camps. I witnessed the reality of Jesus Christ as never before. On the flights back to Hong Kong and then to Hawaii, I was very thankful of my Christian heritage which I had taken for granted. On the layover in Hong Kong, I enjoyed a long hot shower and had more respect for those called to minister in the refugee camps and remote areas of the world proclaiming the reality of Jesus Christ. I arrived back in Kona to spend Christmas with the family in Hawaii.

During our Crossroads DTS, the Lord convicted me of not being a good witness for Him with my chairman when I left the University of Chicago to go to ORU. I reached out to him and found out that the replacement I had found for him had not worked out and had created difficulties for the department. I felt that God was asking me to return to the University of Chicago after the DTS. It was difficult for me, but as I reached out in humility to my former chairman and asked for forgiveness, I felt a burden leave me. Donna and I were prepared to return, but the chairman, Dr. Herbst, at the last minute withdrew an offer to return. I was somewhat disappointed but also relieved to come to a new understanding of how God works. **To go on in Him, we must ask for forgiveness for misrepresentations we have given of Him to others in our zeal to follow Him.** It was then I felt released to follow what God had for me. I felt I had left medicine forever.

Also, God began speaking to me about moving off the YWAM Kona base and buying a home. Living in a Christian community was an important development for us that we had never experienced. However, as a physician, I was always being approached in off hours for medical needs. I understood that those seeking help meant well, but it certainly interfered with our time as a family. Donna and I began praying about buying a house and felt God was leading us to live off base. I found a California-style house in an upscale neighborhood that I really liked and was going to purchase by removing some of my retirement money from the University of Chicago funds. I will never forget that when I prayed about this property, I felt the Lord was telling me that I was expecting too much. A house opened next door to Dr. Bruce Thompson and his wife. This was in a local neighborhood and not up to the standard I had wanted. It would be livable but only had one bathroom. I spoke at a YWAM school in Honolulu for a week, and God told me to possess the land and gave me multiple scriptures (Exodus 20:12-15; Matthew 20:15; and Proverbs 20:15) confirming that the house next to the Thompsons was the one He wanted for us.

We were eventually able to buy the house by using as a down payment money from my contribution to the University of Chicago retirement account plus the motorhome we had left with friends in California. The bank loan was approved since they looked at my previous year employment as a physician and not the income of a missionary living on faith. Only God could have worked that one out. That week in Honolulu was profound. Multiple times God manifested His presence so strongly that everyone was on the floor as He revealed Himself. Never in my life had I seen God manifest Himself so strongly and given such emphatic direction about buying the house. Donna had some reservations about living next to the Thompsons, however.

Donna: There was a time when I felt abandoned and left out as Don was busy ministering and traveling with Bruce. I grew to not like Bruce and was very bitter towards him. Before YWAM I was part of the ministry team with Don, and suddenly in the mission I found myself on the sidelines. I shared my feelings with Dean Sherman, and he told me that I needed to talk to Bruce. I made a written list of twelve grievances I had against him. One day I told the Lord that if He wanted me to share with Bruce I would if I ran into him in the certain area where I was walking to. Sure enough, he was there. I went to him and said, "I don't like you very much, and these are the reasons why," and showed him my list. He said, "Oh, we had better talk about this." We wound up going to the oceanfront and sat on the seawall to discuss my list. To this day I don't remember what I had written, but I do know that there was healing, and today he and his wife, Barbara, are very good friends. Lesson learned—"nip the bud" early so the enemy cannot build upon the platform he is allowed to lay.

Donna in our Hawaii home, 1981

Tredway family in Hawaii (1981). Don, Jennifer (in back), Tamara (next to Donna), Noel (next to Don in front), and Kimberly.

Don: After the DTS, Donna felt the Lord was leading her to attend a second-level school of Foundations in Biblical Counseling at the University of the Nations (UofN), Kona. I applied also but just could not get peace about it and jokingly tell the college today that they never accepted me.

CHAPTER 6

Australia with Dean Sherman

Mark 16:17 These signs will accompany those who have believed: in My name they will cast out demons, they will speak with new tongues.

During our DTS, Dean Sherman shared that he was going back to Australia for a month of ministry in December (1980). As he shared, I felt the Lord was speaking to me to join him. Dean is an accomplished teacher with significant insight into spiritual warfare.[13] I approached Dean and asked if I could travel with him. I could tell he was hesitant since he usually traveled alone.

Coming out of the Charismatic Movement of the late 1970s and ministry times in Tulsa, I came to know the Holy Spirit in a very personal way. I believed in and relied upon the power of God, but I lacked an important principle of God. In **Acts 1:1** Paul relates that Christ did and then taught. Even though I was a teacher in medicine, the Lord was teaching me that any experience that I shared needed to be biblically-based. I found that the combination of sharing my experiences with scripture released more of the power of God. The Lord used Dean Sherman and Bob Yandian to bring me into balance.

When Dean Sherman and I shared with different groups, he would often introduce me as his personal physician. I would get up and say that they needed to pray for him since I was a gynecologist. That was the beginning of a beautiful relationship.

Dean Sherman: I had a trip planned to teach in several places in Australia. I had shared those plans in the CDTS in which you were a student. You approached me one day saying that you thought the Lord had indicated to you that you were to come with me to Australia. I was somewhat uncomfortable with that but agreed to ask the Lord about it. God seemed to confirm it to me. That began an adventure in travel and ministry as well as a lifelong friendship.

You humbly went just to "observe and learn." I took the initiative to ask the various churches, camps, and conferences if you could have some time to minister. Without exception, they expressed that they didn't know you or anything about your ministry so were reluctant to include you. Finally, they each agreed to let you "pray for some people" after I was finished. A couple of times they gave you a session. But each time you simply gave a short testimony from your life or a short message about fear. You asked people to come forward if they wanted prayer. Always only a few, often two or three would come. You would pray and in almost every case, they would fall. Most of the places had never seen or experienced this so it could have hardly been not a genuine function of the Spirit. Each time, after seeing this small miracle, the lines would immediately form with people who wanted to be prayed for. Many were healed in ways they could immediately identify and that inspired many more to come forward. In most cases, almost everybody present was prayed for and experienced healing and being set free from bondage.

The most spectacular incident happened at the YWAM center in Goulburn. I was to teach for the week, morning and evening. Because of a lot of speaking, I had lost my voice. So, I spoke Monday morning but by the end could hardly make a sound. I asked the leaders if you could take the evening session. They were hesitant but agreed. You shared a short message about fear and then asked for people to come up if they wanted to be set free from fear. A line formed down the side of the room. The first two girls you prayed for fell. The third person in the line was a relatively small skinny 18-year-old boy. You took a couple of steps toward him to pray, but then he lunged toward you into animal-like bounds, growling. He punched you in the stomach, picking you off the floor with that punch on one arm, and threw you back about twelve feet. You got up and authoritatively addressed the demonic powers in Jesus' name, which caused the boy to hit the floor like a sack of something. He continued to growl and claw the carpet with his fingers. You began to command spirits to leave him, and he would then calm down some, but then would revive the intensity of the growling and clawing. Some of the staff and students came and formed a circle around you and him and began to sing worship songs. When they sang, the spirits were visibly subdued. When they stopped, the intensity returned. We continued to drive out spirits but without having him totally free. We couldn't think of any other spirits to address, so we asked the Holy Spirit for wisdom. We both felt that he needed to repent, but he was in a semi-conscious state and couldn't. So, we felt the Lord led us to what I had never heard of; we repented for him as an intercession. We said, "If Graeme could, he would repent of _____, _____ and _____." As we spoke that out, being shown by the

Holy Spirit, the powers in him left and he sat up and said, "Where am I? What happened?" He was free and had no memory of what had happened. That was such a demonstration of the Spirit's power and of the need to be led by the Spirit's knowledge and wisdom.

Don: The service described by Dean at the YWAM Center in Goulburn was a pivotal service in my development in the Lord. As I would begin to speak, I could feel the presence of God enter the room and see Him begin to speak to people. When the anointing was present, demon forces would be driven to the surface every time. All one had to do was move in the authority of God at that time and speak forth scripture. That was one of the few times the Lord directed us to stand in the gap and intercede for an individual instead of the individual confessing out his/her sins. It brings to mind the scripture,

> 2 Timothy 2:13 If we are faithless, He remains faithful, for He cannot deny Himself.

We will discuss this more in Appendix D.

Dean taught later in the week about people falling down in the presence of the Lord. This was quite common in the Charismatic Movement and the move of God during the life of Wesley, the Great Awakening with Jonathan Edwards, the ministry of Charles Finney, Titus Cohen during the missionary time in Hawaii, and others. As people recognized the presence of God evident by this sign and wonder, faith would build, and they would seek His presence by going forward for prayer. This will be discussed more in Appendix E.

During that week, I only spoke the first night and Dean taught on what had happened, the power of forgiveness, and the Holy Spirit the rest of the week. I spent the rest of the week meditating on Dean's teaching and was led by the Holy Spirit to study the works of Jesus in the four Gospels. From that study came a teaching on the ministry of Jesus which was later developed into a handbook for teachings in YWAM and the body of Christ. For me, the trips with Bruce Thompson and Dean Sherman were an important time in the development of my walk with God for I learned to be dependent upon Him and not on my own understanding or teaching skills.

> **Proverbs 3:5,6** Trust in the Lord with all your heart, and do not lean on your own understanding. In all your ways acknowledge Him, and He will make your paths straight.

It was during the first few weeks of the DTS that Dean and I taught in Goulburn. Over the years I found that most schools were not ready for a demonstration of the power of God, especially deliverance in Christians, in the first few weeks because of the cessation teachings of some major denominations. It was better for me to speak in the later weeks when there had been teaching on the Holy Spirit. God would also use Donna and me to go into meetings that didn't believe in the gifts to demonstrate His power. Since I was an academic physician, I had credibility, more of that later.

That week in Goulburn with Dean was also important in that I was introduced to YWAM Australia and the national leaders, Tom and Diane Hallas. Tom opened the doors for future trips to Australia and to the FGBMFI, which was to play a major role in our subsequent ministry to Australia, Malaysia, and Indonesia. In addition to becoming a precious friend/coworker in the Lord, Tom also was later ministered to in Kona by Donna, which opened a whole new aspect of ministry. (More later.)

I returned home in February from traveling with Dean. Dr. Bruce Thompson was teaching for a week at a counseling school and asked me to share one day. The day I did, I felt a strong spiritual resistance and challenged the class by saying that God was going to shake them if they didn't heed His voice. At that very moment, there was an earthquake that swayed the building. Suddenly there were demonic manifestations in some of the students. Bruce and I along with the staff then ministered deliverance as the Lord directed. Again, a powerful time in which God confirmed His Word with signs and wonders. What an experience to see God move! Dr. Bruce talks about those early days.

Dr. Bruce Thompson: Dr. Don and Donna (RN) Tredway joined us in the UofN Kona campus Hawaii in 1980. They came as a family from Tulsa, OK, in the USA. Don had been working as the chairman of Obstetrics and Gynecology at ORU. It was such a joy and encouragement to have them join us in the College of Counseling and Health Care (CCHC). It was one of seven colleges in the UofN and had as its vision to take God's Healing to spirit, soul, and body (Sozo) out to the nations. The Tredways became our neighbors and their children, friends with ours. A deep bonding developed between us, and we forged ahead with the vision of pioneering seminars and schools in Hawaii and out among the nations.

Don: As we became established in our new home next to the Thompsons, our girls and their two sons with their dog Sheba became close companions. I also became his associate dean for the College of Counseling and Health Care. I wrote the academic curriculum for the Primary Health Care School and assisted Bruce in the college. It was a fulfilling time as the Lord was using Donna and me to minister to needs on the base and opened opportunities for me to minister internationally.

On the north end of the Island of Hawaii is the small community of Makapala. There was a Christian Retreat Center there that had been given to YWAM. Loren Cunningham, Bruce Thompson, Jeff Littleton (who was running the Counseling Schools), and I met there one weekend to pray for the new College of Counseling and Health Care that had been established. On a previous occasion, a word on base was that the new school would be like a set of twins, Health Care and Counseling. I saw the formation of this college as an extension of prayer and medicine from my time at ORU.

During our time at Makapala, we also felt that the Lord was giving us a blueprint for a clinic that would not only service the base, but eventually branch out to the community, then to the other islands, and then on to the rest of the world. On our way home from the meeting, we drove around the Kona Hospital and claimed it for the Lord. Jeff had a word that I would one day be the administrator. I did not understand that word at that time, but more on that later. My time with these men was a great time of fellowship and a privilege for me. Our fellowship time also included shared cooking and cleanup responsibilities, and even Loren pitched in.

Tom Hallas, the national YWAM director of Australia, visited the Kona base, and Donna and I had an opportunity to meet with him. This meeting resulted in a forerunner of the ministry of God's character in the areas of Jesus as a friend, the Father heart of God, and the maternal side of God's character as it relates to the Holy Spirit.

Tom Hallas: In the 80s I often visited the Kona campus of the University of the Nations to minister to students doing the basic YWAM Discipleship Training Course (DTS). I had been ministering all day and was a little exhausted and had an evening social meeting with Dr. Don and Donna Tredway. I had heard of their ministry but had not met them personally. Don had ministered in Australia with Dean Sherman, a YWAM leader with whom I had been associated since the late 60s.

Dean had done several ministry trips with Don and was deeply impressed with the simplicity and naturalness of the way the gifts of the Spirit seemed to be evidenced through Don's life.

No big fanfare or energetic buildup but just a very relational flow of words of knowledge and grace to deliver and heal.

As I had a special interest in the ministry of inner healing, our evening quickly started with a conversation with that focus. I had been on a personal journey towards wholeness and spoke and ministered about the Father heart of God. Years earlier I had fully reconciled with my own father in relation to his model of authority and its negative impact on my life.

However, this evening's conversation moved toward my infant days when I was separated from my mother after my traumatic birth that left her gravely ill. It wasn't until years later and two more births that she received surgery to repair the damage caused by my birth.

Don and Donna seemed to have a special grace of concern and compassion come upon them as we talked about those of my infant years.

Donna felt that she should pray for me and hold me in her arms like my mother would. A very new idea for me even though some years previously a dear brother and friend, Jack Winter, who in many ways had introduced me to the Father heart message, had held me in his arms and prayed into the love deprivation that I had incurred due to unfulfilled expectation and need because of Dad's fathering manner.

The scripture came to my mind: "As a mother comforts so I will comfort you says the Lord." Also blessed be the Father of mercies and the God of all comfort.

My anxiety as an adult male being held in a mothering embrace was somewhat minimized by these scriptural reminders. However, there was still a choice to become as a little child, humble myself, and receive the ministry of God's grace through Donna's prayer ministry.

I was suddenly asleep for how long I do not know, but when I was awakened Donna was still holding me.

A whole new world of the complimentary grace of God's mothering care dawned on my thinking about the wholeness of God and the need of maternal deprivation finding an answer in God's mothering care.

I now had ground and gramma to further serve my fellow human beings in their journey toward wholeness.

Forward thirty years the Tredways are staying with Di and me in our home in Canberra, Australia. Six days of catching up and a day of ministry at the YWAM Base.

Donna: I don't remember anything specific about ministering to Tom except that when I cradled him in my arms the Lord "took him away in the Spirit" to do a great work of emotional and spiritual healing. I held him like a baby for approximately five hours as God worked. Don was there in the room and became a bit anxious about the length of time it was taking. He had no understanding as to what was happening, so I prayed and asked the Lord to put him to sleep too. God is faithful. He did. They both "woke up" at the same time.

Don: After teaching with Bruce in the Counseling School at Makapala for the first time, I spoke there yearly from 1981 to 1994. We also became a part of Calvary Community Church in Kona, encouraging the pastor, David Rees Thomas. I would speak occasionally for the Sunday morning services, and through his association with the parent church in San Jose, California, I was invited to speak at a clinic they held. I was able to spend time with one of the major speakers, Jack Hayford, from Church on the Way in Los Angeles. Again, God allowed me to meet and sit under the teachings of another one of His anointed servants.

During the next few years, Donna and I would travel with Pastor Wilkerson. As he ministered, God would give me words of knowledge **(1 Corinthians 12:8)** just before Pastor Wilkerson spoke the same word that would minister to people. While I worked with Dr. Wilkerson, Donna and others would walk among the congregation and be drawn to individuals that God was ministering to.

Donna: As I would walk among the people, God would indicate an individual that He wanted to minister to. I can't explain just how it happened except to say that it was just an inward knowing. He would either have me pray for them where they were or bring them forward to be prayed for up front.

Don: As I look back, the times with Pastor Wilkerson were amazing and an important time in my spiritual growth. He had a tremendous sense of the convicting power of the Holy Spirit. At times we would go into what seemed to be the deadest church with minimal praise and worship. He would get up to preach and would say that God is going to save so many people. He would proclaim that a certain number of people needed to come forward to accept the Lord Jesus Christ. I at times was certain he had missed it, but he would just begin thanking the Lord. He would also challenge Christians in the congregation to believe with him and would repeat "Thank you, Lord" again and again. Sometimes it seemed to take a while, but knowing that God spoke to him, he would not let go. Eventually, the convicting power of the Holy Spirit would fall, and people would come forward crying and repenting of their sins. I have never known anyone who knew more of the convicting power of the Holy Spirit than Pastor Wilkerson. I thought it was just for his ministry until one day the Lord asked me to do the same. We are to be imitators of Christ! Again and again God showed me how He used other ministers for the purpose of building faith in me so that when the day came, I would be prepared to flow in the ministry of the Holy Spirit.

CHAPTER 7

Return to
Australia with
YWAM and FGBMFI

Mark 16:20 And they went out and preached everywhere, while the Lord worked with them, and confirmed the word by the signs that followed.

After my trip to Australia with Dean in March 1981, I returned to Tulsa for a brief visit in April. My pastor, Bob Yandian, at our home church, Grace Fellowship, was teaching on Romans[14] which was profound. I was asked to share at a Sunday evening service. I was only to share for a few minutes, but God had me start sharing about curses and abominations. The Spirit of the Lord started moving for the next hour with many being set free. What a wonderful confirmation of God's presence in our home church.

Return to Australia with YWAM and FGBMFI During 1981 and 1982

John 12:26 If anyone serves Me, he must follow Me; and where I am, there My servant will be also; if anyone serves Me, the Father will honor him.

I received an invitation from Tom Hallas to return to Australia to teach at a DTS in the Blue Mountains outside of Sydney. I was excited that God was opening new doors. Before my going to Australia, during times of ministry the Lord at times would give me words of knowledge about curses, curses that an individual had brought on themselves and of generational curses. It did not make sense to me, but as I prayed for individuals with authority, I witnessed God setting people free. I then began to study the subject more and God gave me a teaching on it (see Appendix C).

At that DTS in the Blue Mountains, I taught on the subject in depth for the first time. As soon as I began sharing on the abomination of bestiality (**Leviticus 18:23**), the Holy Spirit told me to stop for the day and have the students pray about what had been discussed. For the remainder of the day, I fasted and went before the Lord because I questioned what I had done. The next morning the room was very quiet. When we started, I asked if anyone had anything to share. Two young married men shared that they had had intercourse with an animal. One had been with a German shepherd dog and the other with a sheep. Both men had feelings of being unclean and both had difficulties in their marriage. Neither were filled with the Holy Spirit although they had been seeking it. They had been afraid to share because they felt that they would be rejected. The two had shared and prayed with their wives for the first time the night before, and both asked the Lord for forgiveness. There was no rejection from the class as they shared, only love and acceptance as members of the class gathered around them. Both were released in the Holy Spirit as the class prayed for them. Through this situation I began to see how important God's Word and ordinances are in our lives and the significance of the cross and resurrection of Jesus. Peter Brownhill and his wife were leaders of the DTS at the time. Peter shares his impression of that event.

Peter Brownhill, YWAM Perth WA: In 1981 in New South Wales, my wife and I were running a Discipleship Training School. It was being run in the Blue Mountains at a retreat centre.

When I talk about this period of time it was after Shirl and I had experienced a season in our lives of being trained cross-culturally in discipleship with the mission we were with. We were and still are with Youth with a Mission.

One of the speakers who came to us, organized through our leaders Tom Hallas and his good friend Dean Sherman, was Dr. Donald Tredway. Being a recognized obstetrician, I really wasn't sure about how the week was going to go. However, Dr. Don arrived and felt the Lord impressing upon him topics that related to generational curses. So, I felt God was up to something. The group I was leading was thirty-eight in number including staff. The week was characterized by teaching on how the enemy can gain satanic footholds in people's lives through parents, grandparents, and great-grandparents' involvements in various areas of witchcraft and idolatry.

When the Holy Spirit was given freedom to move and be applied in individuals' lives, there was a visible move of the Holy Spirit in individuals beyond anything I had ever known up till that time of my life. One of the generational curses brought over people's lives was that of Freemasonry. This also involved witchcraft, infirmity, and pain in their lives. One particular guy had been involved strongly in taking and dealing drugs. When he was being ministered to, the power of God would come upon him strongly. He would be in a state of being totally set free from the bondages of being in crime, drugs, and underworld crimes.

The Masonic was not the only issue but also deep generational curses of unforgiveness and bitterness. The week was a visible tangible look at New Testament Christianity in action. It was so educational, and consequently I was tooled up in being aware of the supernatural. Together with other speakers who also were mentoring me in deliverance, it was a part of my discipling toolbox that got filled up that was not there up till that time.

I am forever grateful to the Lord for bringing Dr. Don into my life. This episode was back in 1981. A toolbox I felt for ministry and discipleship got filled up to equip others in areas related to setting people free from the demonic.

Don: Peter related to areas of Masonic curses. Those curses were also strongholds in my life that will be discussed later. It was exciting again to see God confirm His Word with signs and wonders during that DTS. I then returned to the US.

For a total of three weeks toward the end of April and into May 1981, Donna and I ministered at the Regional FGBMFI meeting in Houston, Texas, the YWAM Tyler base also in Texas, our home church, Grace Fellowship in Tulsa, and Bethany Church in Hacienda Heights, California, along with a stop at Melodyland before returning to Kona.

The time at the Tyler base was profound. We had come from the Houston meeting and were to speak at the DTS for a week.

There God revealed Himself to us in a new way. We started with an evening meeting. The DTS leader introduced me, and I read a scripture about God revealing Himself. A young girl on the front row fell on the floor screaming, "Daddy, don't hit me." Donna and I ministered to her and then such cries started happening to others in the room. One young lady got up and ran out of the room into a nearby field. Donna ran after her, pointed to her, and said, "Stop in the name of Jesus." She fell to the ground like a puppet being cut off its strings. The young lady returned to the meeting where she experienced ministry and freedom. The whole evening was like that, total ministry after opening in prayer and reading a scripture about God revealing Himself.

The base was not accustomed to a move of the Holy Spirit like that. Several hours into the meeting the DTS leader was noticeably uncomfortable. He came forward to close the meeting and said, "We want to thank Dr. Tredway." As soon as he touched my shoulder, he was slain in the Spirit and fell to the floor. The ministry continued. What an exciting time of teaching and God demonstrating His power that week. **Acts 1:1** was fulfilled.

> **Acts 1:1** The first account I composed, Theophilus, about all that Jesus **began to do and teach** (my emphasis).

The FGBMFI invited me back to Australia. Again, there were more powerful times in the Lord where His presence filled the room. I had been invited by a precious friend in the Lord, an engineer, David Grantham. David relates what he witnessed the Lord do at a weekend retreat.

David Grantham. An FGBMFI weekend in June 1981 was held at a Christian site called Merroo approximately 50 km from Sydney.

There were 140 people attending from around the state. Dr. Don Tredway was the main speaker on Saturday night, and there was a real presence of the Holy Spirit in the meeting. Part of Don's message was relating to a Christian's weapons in standing against demonic oppression, particularly the name of Jesus and the blood of the Lamb. Also, Christians were to have nothing to do with the occult; several items were mentioned including Freemasonry. Immediately a woman ran screaming out of the meeting. A call was made for those who needed prayer for deliverance, and around 20 or more responded. Following a period of intense ministry, many were released and set free. The lady that ran out of the meeting had a father who was very heavily involved with Freemasonry and was wonderfully set free. Several people accepted the Lord and received the gift of the Holy Spirit, a great weekend that glorified the Lord.

Don: I also spoke at an FGBMFI North Queensland convention in Mackay on June 25-27, 1981. The Lord had me speak again on curses and Freemasonry. An Anglican priest came forward for prayer to receive the infilling of the Holy Spirit. He related that he had sought it for a long time but that there seemed to be a block. He also related that he was involved in Freemasonry. That night the Holy Spirit revealed to him that Freemasonry was the block and he had put a curse upon himself. He then confessed and asked for forgiveness for his involvement. He rebuked any effect of it upon his life. I agreed and prayed with him. He immediately felt a release, was filled with the Holy Spirit, and began speaking in tongues. Over the years I have seen many Christians in bondage due to Freemasonry. That will be discussed in depth in Appendix C.

Returning to Kona from Australia, I spent a week teaching at a DTS in the YWAM Honolulu base. They had asked me to speak on deliverance since there was little teaching on the subject at the time. They had also invited the staff of Teen Challenge Honolulu to attend. I will never forget that week. It was a week of clinical demonstrations. I would give examples of what I had seen in Asia, such as dedication of children to idols and what scripture had to say. When I mentioned that, a young Indian lady screamed and fell to the floor moving across it like a snake. We found out that she had been dedicated to the snake god. The presence of God filled the room like a cloud, and the anointing of the Holy Spirit set her free. Oh, what a change in her. She now had a countenance about her face of peace and joy, rejoicing in what the Lord had done. All week was like that. There were many demonic manifestations and God setting His people free through the power of His Spirit as the Word went forth. It was one of the most exciting weeks in my walk with God.

> **2 Corinthians 3:17** Now the Lord is the Spirit, and where the Spirit of the Lord is, there is liberty.

After I returned to Kona, I received another call from David Grantham asking me to speak at the FGBMGI meetings in Australia June, July, and August. I left June 10 and Donna joined me July 1st after leaving the children at my parents' farm in southern Illinois for the summer. The children were excited since this was their first time off the island since we went to Hawaii. I spoke sixty-one times and had enough lamb to eat for a lifetime. God continued to powerfully manifest Himself during those meetings and brought forth many freedoms and healings.

When Donna travels with me, the anointing is stronger. The Bible speaks about a husband and wife being of one flesh (**Genesis 2:24**). I believe that is true spiritually as well. The two of us together in agreement gives us a better clarity of how the Holy Spirit wants to move. She has a gift of discernment that God uses to point out people that He wants to touch in a special way. She will spend more time with them going deeper into their history by talking to them and praying for them on a more one-on-one basis.

> Matthew 18:19 Again I say to you, that if two of you agree on earth about anything that they may ask, it shall be done for them by My Father who is in heaven.

One high point of that trip was being asked to speak to an academic medical group of about forty physicians at a hotel in Sydney on July 4, 1981. There I met Dr. Ernest Crocker, a nuclear medicine physician who later became a precious friend and one that I would travel with to China on medical teaching trips. Dr. Crocker wrote regarding our times together in his book.[15] Below is his account of what happened at the meeting.

Dr. Ernest Crocker: We first met in Sydney at your presentation to doctors at the Sydney Hilton. Can't recall the date but it would have been a year before our first trip to China together. I think we met at Dave Grantham's house, and I still remember the cowboy boots that you wore that night.

The meeting at the Hilton was scheduled through the FGBMFI by David Grantham. A general invitation had gone out to Christian doctors, and the presentation was arranged for a Saturday afternoon in the Hilton Ballroom, Pitt St Sydney. I was the chair that afternoon. I was just a young doctor at the time and quite young in the Spirit. I was a bit concerned about what might be said and how my professors who were staunch evangelicals might respond.

The meeting was well attended. The hierarchy of Sydney's Christian medical profession were present. Your presentation was not what I believe might have been anticipated by many. You spoke quietly, clearly, and rationally about your professional experience, your healing, and your faith. Printed curriculum was available by the entrance door.

At the conclusion of your presentation, you invited people to come forward for prayer largely for their practices. Many streamed forward. And before long many of them had hit the deck. Dr. Graeme Hughes (now emeritus Prof Graeme Hughes from the Royal Hospital for Women) and I were somewhat astounded to see the wife of the O&G professor sprawled on the floor in her rather expensive fur stole. On the right side of the ballroom someone began to manifest. I rushed across in front of you to help. As I did so you raised your hand, my knees buckled, and I ended up on the floor. This was interesting as just a few weeks prior I had been prayed for by Kenneth Hagin in Scot's Church in the city. I had gone up onto the stage and joined the prayer line. When he prayed for me, I felt him pushing me backward. I resisted. I thought, "You are not going to push me over. If this is for real, I want to know about it."

"You're resisting, you're resisting," he said. And he was right. No one was going to push me over. So, I had a few doubts about falling down in the Spirit after that night. But not after the afternoon in the Hilton ballroom.

There were many other meetings of course. One I remember was at a services club in Epping, no longer there. During ministry, you held up your arm over one side of the congregation. Nearly all of them fell down.

Don: Donna and I were able to connect again with Noel and Phyl Gibson while we were in Australia and stayed with them in their condominium in Drummoyne, NSW. They also happened to be friends of Dr. Ern Crocker. The Gibsons accompanied us to another FGBMFI dinner meeting where I was to speak. During the meal, both Noel and I came under an attack of the enemy. Noel became confused, and I thought that he may have suffered a minor stroke. I was then introduced by David Grantham, and when I stood to speak, I also became confused, felt oppressed, and had difficulty focusing my eyes. From memory, I started reciting:

> **Isaiah 61:1** The Spirit of the Lord GOD is upon me, because the LORD has anointed me to bring good news to the afflicted; He has sent me to bind up the broken hearted, to proclaim liberty to captives and freedom to prisoners.

As soon as I spoke that verse, the oppression broke, and the Holy Spirit gave me words of knowledge about healing. Then we moved into a time of ministry and teaching fulfilling **Acts 1:1** where Christ did and then taught. Many were set free from demonic oppression that night. I was exhausted afterward, and Noel's mind cleared. We both knew we had been under an attack of the enemy and sought the Lord asking what the dent in our armor was that allowed the enemy to attack us. A couple of weeks later we drove by the venue during the day and noticed that it was a Masonic lodge. Then we received the understanding. Noel had a family history of relatives being involved in Freemasonry and so did I. My father was a Shriner, a division of the Masons, and was part of a scooter motor patrol. I never had an interest in joining the Masons. During my father's funeral, his Shriner friends came and placed the Shriner apron and accessories in the casket. Noel shared with me in depth the occult bondages that result from Freemasonry, and over the next few years, the Lord would pass on additional infor-mation.[16-20] I find it interesting that the Lord was having me share on curses and would reveal this family curse to me that gave the enemy an opening in my armor that night. Although neither of us had been personally involved in Freemasonry, we thanked God for the revelation and asked for forgiveness for our relatives and forefathers who had been involved and rebuked any curse upon our lives and that of our families. The Holy Spirit also convicted me to burn my father's personal masonic items that had been given to me by my mother. Donna and I would burn those upon our return to Tulsa the next year.

In August of 1981, we headed back to California from Australia via Honolulu where we had an overnight stay. We attended the annual Charismatic Clinic at Melodyland in Anaheim where I was asked to speak in one of the breakout sessions. The Lord had me speak on fear. At the beginning of the session, He told me to have a lady in the front row stand and to pray for her. As I started to pray, she was slain in the Spirit and lay on the floor during the whole lecture. At the end of the class, she got up and shared that she had been blind in one eye but now could see. She had been in the presence of God during the class and He healed her inwardly of various things in her life. **Just to come into the presence of God brings healing.** What a privilege it is to serve Him.

Also, that year I was teaching on healing and praying for backs when Donna felt that God wanted to do something unusual.

Donna: Don and I had been to a healing service sometime prior to our time at Melodyland and saw a pastor pray for people with back problems in a unique way. He would have them stand and instructed them to plant their feet and to follow the promptings of the Holy Spirit as to how He wanted to move them (swaying, bending, stretching, etc.). During one of the teaching sessions at

Melodyland, I was sitting in the audience as Don was praying for people. He prayed for a lady with back problems who was slain in the Spirit and fell right in front of me. I knew that God wasn't finished with her and knew what He wanted to do. I nudged the friend that I was sitting next to and told her what I was sensing. On her third nudge, she told me to tell Don. I did and Don told me to go ahead and pray for her. I stood the lady up and gave her instructions to follow the promptings of the Holy Spirit as He would lead her. Others came forward for prayer and soon many in the room were swaying, bending, twisting, stretching, etc. as they followed God's prompts.

Don: I must admit this experience was strange. Was this a sign and a wonder or was this the enemy trying to deceive us? Some of the church elders came to the second session and observed this phenomenon happening again. They later came to us sharing that they didn't believe this was of God, and we were told not to let it happen again. Don't ever think that you can put God in a box.

The next day the presence of the Lord filled the room and there was a spontaneous outbreak of the same manifestation during the teaching session. A senior elder, a precious woman of God, was there who had severe back problems. As we prayed, the same phenomenon happened to her, and she was healed. At the closing session of the Charismatic Clinic, Pastor Wilkerson publicly acknowledged that God was at work in our lives with signs and wonders. It was a lesson for us, however, that we must examine and make sure that everything is done according to Scripture and results in people going deeper in God.

From Anaheim, we traveled to Alabama for the Regional FGBMFI meeting in Birmingham. God had me teach on curses and the stronghold of the Masons. There was a wonderful move of the Spirit, and many were set free. I recall being rebuked by a man in line who was a Mason. The message on curses and abominations has become a powerful tool in revealing curses that we may have brought upon ourselves through our own involvement and the generational effects upon our children.

God also opened the doors for me to travel for a month to minister in Norway, Germany, and Switzerland.

October 8-10, 1981, I returned to Australia to speak at the regional FGBMFI meeting in Toowoomba, Queensland, a beautiful area of Australia about 80 miles west of Brisbane. I was one of two speakers at the convention. Sir Lionel Luckhoo was the other. He was a Guyanese politician, diplomat, and well-known lawyer famed for his 245 consecutive successful defenses in murder cases. Sir Lionel Luckhoo was the brother of the last governor-general of Guyana, Sir Edward Luckhoo, and quite a celebrity in the British Commonwealth. He had a powerful personal testimony of becoming a believer in Jesus Christ. We were quite a pair, a doctor and a lawyer. I could not pass up the opportunity to share that only God could get a doctor and lawyer together.

Sir Lionel was quite a speaker as you could imagine. His sincere love for the Lord touched my heart, and I know that God did some healing to my heart concerning lawyers. Perhaps the healing was to prepare me for what was to come in the legal arena.

It was a powerful three-day conference, and I was exhausted by the time of the closing banquet. Sir Lionel was the speaker, and I enjoyed his testimony and challenge during his address. When he was halfway through the allotted time for the speech, he told the attendees, "Now Dr. Tredway will finish out our night." I was surprised. I was just expecting to join him later to pray for people. Someone had forgotten to inform me that we were both sharing, either that or I had missed it. As in my university professorship, I would always spend time preparing, but not that night.

As I got up before the crowd of a few hundred people, I was really praying saying, "Lord, I need You." I will never forget what happened as I reached the podium. I felt the presence of the Holy Spirit at my side, and He began to give me words of knowledge and prophecy for various individuals. People would come forward as I called them out. Some would not even get to the front because the presence of the Lord would come upon them in a dramatic way, and they were slain in the Spirit without having hands laid on them. For others, the slightest touch released the power of God to come upon them. Faith arose in the room, and it was electric. People spontaneously came forward for prayer as Sir Lionel and I prayed late into the night. Sir Lionel was so excited because the same anointing fell upon him. It was a glorious time. It was the Lord. He is so faithful if we are just obedient to be where He wants us to be. I felt so fulfilled in the Lord that night and better understood what the apostle Paul meant when he wrote:

> **2 Timothy 4:2** preach the word; be ready in season and out of season; reprove, rebuke, exhort, with great patience and instruction.

Toowomba, Australia Regional Convention, October 1981. Dr. Tredway seated, second to left of center.

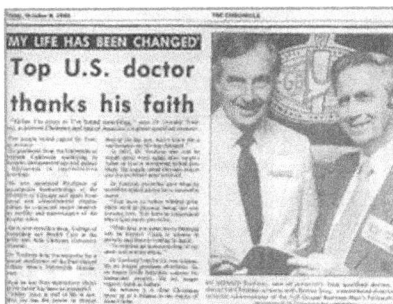

Local Australian newspaper notice of FGBMFI Regional Meeting, Toowoomba, 1981.

Dr. Tredway at FGBMFI Toowomba, Australia Regional Convention, 1981.

CHAPTER 8

Malaysia, Singapore, and Indonesia

Matthew 28:18-20 And Jesus came up and spoke to them, saying, "All authority has been given to Me in heaven and on earth. Go therefore and make disciples of all the nations, baptizing them in the name of the Father and the Son and the Holy Spirit, teaching them to observe all that I commanded you; and lo, I am with you always, even to the end of the age."

In addition to Australia, ministry opportunities with the FGBMFI also opened in Malaysia and Indonesia. We had multiple trips to Malaysia where a group of Chinese physicians associated with the FGBMFI were being used by the Lord all throughout Malaysia. Again, the Lord used signs and wonders to establish His authority and to bring many into the kingdom. Many of those sessions we have on videotape. As I review them, I relive those times in God. At times the Lord would have me start a meeting by pointing to people in the audience, have them stand, and the Lord would give me a word for them. As I gave the word they would start weeping and fall under the presence of the Lord. Then His authority would be established, and the audience would be open to receive what the Lord had to say. God gave us favor in Australia and Malaysia, and doors opened for us to share in churches. The people wanted to hear from an academic physician who believed in healing and moved in signs and wonders.

On one trip to Malaysia, Donna and I were praying for individuals at an evening meeting when a lady came forward who had a severe skin rash. Donna had a word about a curse. We then prayed claiming the blood of Jesus Christ to break the curse. The next morning her husband called us and invited us for lunch. He shared that when his wife woke up, the rash was gone. He was a government official who oversaw the public water facility in the town. He had a very luxurious house and served us a very nice lunch. The lady related that she had the rash for seven years, and had been to Singapore and London to see specialists, but they were unable to help her. We asked what had happened seven years ago. She related that at that time they had fired a Chinese maid who had left angrily and left small papers in the house with Chinese scripts. As we prayed about these papers, we had the understanding that they were curses. The power of the blood of Jesus broke the curse. This was an eye-opening event for us considering our Western training.

We had a similar situation in Singapore where we were asked to pray for an infant with a severe medical illness. Word of knowledge indicated that it was a curse. We went to the home where they related a similar story of firing a housemaid who had left papers with curses on the infant's crib. We again prayed claiming the blood of Jesus Christ on the child, rebuked the curse, and burned the papers. We were informed later that the child was healed when they returned to their physician. With all my medical training I had never considered illness because of a curse. The Holy Spirit was continuing to teach Donna and myself. (See Appendix E and Derek Prince's excellent discussion[18])

We also traveled to Eastern Malaysia (old Borneo) and stayed in a hotel in Sibu. We had to leave the windows open because the smell of sewer gas filled the room. There were no traps in the plumbing, so we wet towels and put them over the drains to help keep the gas from coming up. This was also an area where people wore heavy metal rings in their ears to stretch their earlobes that at times would reach almost to the edge of the shoulder. (I had a fear that my hands might get caught in their ears during prayer lines.) Also, this was once the region of headhunters. The longhouses still had shrunken heads hanging from the beams.

In the church, there was wonderful music, and the men and women sat on different sides of the sanctuary. As we shared, the Spirit of the Lord filled the room and the Holy Spirit ministered with prophetic words and demonstrations of His presence by people falling under God's power. Many were touched as Donna and I prayed. The Lord only showed us some of what He was doing. One had a sense that He was healing not only physically but inwardly as well, with tears running down their faces. From Sibu we traveled to Kuchung in East Malaysia where we had the same experience. Praise the Lord for His faithfulness and loving-kindness.

Psalm 136:23 (AMP) To Him Who [earnestly] remembered us in our low estate and imprinted us [on His heart], for His mercy and loving-kindness endure forever.

During our visit to Eastern Malaysia, we were asked to go and pray for a man in the hospital. Below is Donna's account of that event.

Donna: Before leaving Kona for this trip, I had a feeling that God was going to do something big and even wondered if we would see Him raise the dead. In Eastern Malaysia we were asked to visit and pray for a man who had been involved in an automobile accident. He was clinically dead and not expected to live. The family had been called in to be at his side. On the way to the "hospital," I felt that the Lord wanted us to visit this man and pray for him every day that we were there. We did so. The first day Don stood and prayed at the man's side while I was at his feet. When Don started to pray, the man turned his head towards him. I was excited and fully expected the man to rise and jump out of bed, but he didn't. It wasn't until we left the city that we were told what happened. The day after we left the man "woke up" with his arms raised, singing and praising the Lord. I asked God why we didn't see the miracle happen when we prayed for him, and God said, "You would have taken the credit."

Don: One of my trips to Malaysia was very challenging for me. Just before I was to leave, my church in Kona prayed for me at the Sunday morning service. That afternoon one of the church elders came to see me and said that he had a word for me. I could tell he was troubled. He said, "Don, do not go for the Lord has told me that if you do, you will die." That was shocking because I had felt for a long time that the Lord shared with me that I would die during a time of ministry. The elder was a respected businessman in the community and one that I trusted. Donna and I prayed but felt I should still go. All during the trip that word was in the back of my mind as well as what I felt the Lord had spoken.

I recall one situation in East Malaysia that I will never forget. When I got up to speak, I felt an extreme degree of oppression. It was a true demonic attack. The Lord showed me a witch doctor toward the rear of the auditorium. I confronted him in the name of the Lord, and as I pointed my finger at him, he was flung over two rows of chairs by the power of God. With that, most of the people rushed forward seeking God. I felt that I would be crushed, but a precious brother from Singapore protected me. It was Vincent, a former member of the Chinese Tong who had been used of the Lord in Indonesia. Vincent had gone to one of the remote islands of Indonesia where they would give poison to a stranger coming into the village. He went knowing what to expect and survived the test. He then shared the gospel and had a move of God in the village. I thank the Lord for Vincent for he certainly knew how to control crowds.

The final meeting of this trip was a regional Asian FGBMFI convention in Singapore. As I got up to share, the Lord showed me multiple attendees who would be martyrs. The spontaneous message He had me speak that afternoon was "Are You Willing to Die for Jesus." I had never thought of the ultimate sacrifice. The experience that I had on this trip was all in preparation for the message at this meeting. All those whom God showed me would be martyrs answered the call that day. Our ultimate identification with Christ would be to be like Jesus, who knew His death would come. I have a better understanding now of the martyrs in Hebrews 11. As servants of Jesus Christ, are we willing to be martyrs for our faith in Him?

In January 1982, Donna and I plus the four girls were invited to travel to New Zealand, Australia, Malaysia, and Singapore. We needed a teacher for the girls, so we asked a friend who was a teacher, Ginger Burnside, along with her daughter, Shelly (the same age as our second oldest), to travel with us. It was good to travel as a family because my first year in YWAM, I had traveled alone and was gone for half of the year. Our children were able to see how God was using us, and they also participated at times by singing before I shared the Word. The girls were exposed to various aspects of the mission field, including squatty potties. We took a train from Penang to Kuala Lumpur, which was quite an experience for all of us. I felt like a tour guide, especially at airports, with a group of seven females and all the luggage. We still talk about those experiences.

Thank you, Lord, for showing Your faithfulness to my family.

In December of 1981, the Lord began speaking to me about returning to medicine. I was very fulfilled in ministry but knew ministry would always be a part of my life. Donna and I both felt that we would be moving again and began to seek and wait for God's guidance.

In 1982 Donna traveled with me without the girls to Kuala Lumpur, Malaysia. The FGBMFI had scheduled a Full Gospel Rally at a major hotel, WISMA MCA, on April 3, of that year. A few hundred people attended. I had a sense that God wanted to do something special and fasted the whole day. God told me that I would see something that I had never seen before. I could get nothing else from Him. Even as we were worshiping at the beginning of the evening service, I had nothing. This would happen from time to time, and I would just trust the Lord to speak as I opened my mouth. I was praying silently as I was introduced and went to the podium. I began in prayer. The Lord gave me some words of knowledge about healing and then released me into a long prophecy. From the prophecy, I went into a message in tongues for fifteen to twenty minutes. It was as if I was having an out-of-body experience and I was looking down at my body. As

I spoke, the presence of God filled the room, and all through the audience people began falling down, screaming, and being set free of demonic forces. Many of the people in attendance were of Indian heritage from India. Then the Lord gave me the interpretation in English for another fifteen to twenty minutes, and others in the audience were also set free from demons. Then the Lord had me give an invitation for salvation. Most of the people came forward to receive Jesus as Lord. After praying the sinner's prayer, the Lord had me point to a large Indian man who then began staggering, twisting, and fell on the floor and was delivered of demonic forces as we took authority over generational curses. What a time in God! I was told later that I spoke a Hindu dialect. Praise the Lord, Scripture was fulfilled that night. God's glory draws people to Himself, and His power brings healing and freedom as He sets people free. I was exhausted after that but so fulfilled in God.

> **Acts 2:3-6 (AMP)** There appeared to them tongues resembling fire, which were being distributed [among them], and they rested on each one of them [as each person received the Holy Spirit]. And they were all filled [that is, diffused throughout their being] with the Holy Spirit and began to speak in other tongues (different languages), as the Spirit was giving them the ability to speak out [clearly and appropriately].
>
> Now there were Jews living in Jerusalem, devout and God-fearing men from every nation under heaven. And when this sound was heard, a crowd gathered, and they were bewildered because each one was hearing those in the upper room speaking in his own language or dialect.

We finished up the trip with Dr. Bruce at a seminar in Singapore in June 1982 where we helped Bruce in ministry.

Dr. Bruce Thompson: One of our early seminars was with the Singapore FGBMFI. Pastors, counsellors, medical professionals, and others attended. I was teaching on the "Divine Plumb Line" along with team testimonies. It was a very attentive group, and we felt God's anointing on the seminar.

An invitation was given for those who wanted to come out and have prayer. As I prayed, prayers for repentance were spoken out, and then Don and Dona followed up. God's Spirit rested heavily upon them, and soon there was a lineup of people slain in the Spirit lying on the floor. Some participants were so struck that they ran out of the meeting in fear but slowly returned to be touched by the Lord in powerful ways. Some manifested signs of demonization and experienced deliverance as the Tredways prayed with them. This was a turning point in the seminar and people became so open and hungry for God. Healings, and deliverances continued through the week with meetings going on to midnight. God was not only moving among the participants but also in our team as we saw God move in such powerful ways.

Don: Loren Cunningham was in Singapore a short time after the Singapore meeting with Dr. Bruce. He related how the Lord used that conference to radically change the medical community in Singapore.

Donna did a lot of counseling on the base in Kona while I was gone. The Lord used her in inner healing and deliverance, and when I was in town we would often work together. There was no sound-proofing in any of the rooms we used (island-style construction), so we would pray that the Lord would deafen ears during times of ministry if there was any commotion.

Malaysia, Singapore, and Indonesia

There were two deliverances during that time that I will always remember. One involved a DTS student who had a great fear of water. It affected her so much that she even had a hard time taking a bath. As we prayed, the Lord showed us a man floating on a large section of wood in the ocean after a ship had sunk. As we questioned the girl, she related the story of a distant relative who had been involved in a shipwreck. We prayed and broke the generational curse, and she was set free from the fear of water.

The other incident involved a fellow that we were taking through deliverance. The demon spoke and said that he couldn't leave (we usually do not converse since they are liars). It said that it had too much baggage and couldn't. We responded that you do not have suitcases and commanded it to go in the name of Jesus Christ. It left.

I returned to Malaysia in June 1982 and was accompanied by my neighbor from Oakland, California, Rick Gamble. He and his family had followed us to YWAM Kona where they did a Crossroads DTS. He and I shared in Kuala Lumpur at the Abundant Life Center, and again God moved in ministry to His people.

I was invited back to Malaysia and Indonesia by the FGBMFI and to YWAM New Zealand and Australia in December 1982. Before the trip, the Lord spoke to me that I was not discipling by not taking someone with me. I felt led to invite a Nazarene minister, Ralph Knepper, who was in the Counseling Department at YWAM Kona. Ralph was a precious brother in the Lord who was growing in the Holy Spirit. Donna and I had worked with Ralph where he was a counselor for the community and the YWAM staff. He moved very well in words of knowledge but had not experienced the power of God that Donna and I experienced. God had challenged me that I should be taking people with me so that they could be released in the Holy Spirit.

Over the years I found that as I asked individuals to travel and assist me in ministry, they would be changed by the anointing. It was true with Ralph. While he felt his gift was in counseling, the Lord began to release him during times of ministry to move with the anointing in praying for others. I left him for a week in Australia to minister in a YWAM counseling school while I traveled to teach at a DTS in New Zealand. From there we both traveled to Ipoh, Malaysia, to a relatively new YWAM base that had been established by a young physician and his wife. They were a precious couple that opened their home to us. Ralph and I ministered in a local church and to the small YWAM DTS group. Again, God would manifest Himself, and I could see Ralph growing more confident in the Lord.

It was so hot in Ipoh during the afternoons. To help refresh us, we were introduced to the wonderful treat of Malaysian Ice Kacang. It is a very popular refreshing dessert commonly sold by street vendors. It consists of sweet-tasting shaved ice with numerous toppings such as red beans, creamy sweet corn, grass jelly, palm nut, etc. What a wonderful treat for a hot summer day.

Ralph and I then traveled to Kuala Lumpur where we were to minister at a Full Gospel Rally. I had been to Kuala Lumpur before with Dr. Peter Tong at the Abundant Life Center and at the largest church, Full Gospel Assembly (FGA) where we experienced major moves of God. There was an air of expectancy at the rally, and the Spirit of the Lord moved mightily. God released Ralph in deliverance as we were praying in the prayer line. He became as excited as the attendees. The people were aware of the power of the enemy, and when they saw God delivering people of demonic forces, they would flock forward for salvation, healing, and deliverance. In fact, we had such a move of God that the group in Malaysia that had invited us delayed my trip to Indonesia and scheduled extra meetings. In the Asian culture, loss of face or shame is a strong area of bondage. We witnessed the Lord setting many free from this stronghold (see Appendix B).

Ralph went on to Indonesia to start the planned meetings before I got there. He had the confidence that the power of God was with him. (I still remember Ralph's eyes the first time he prayed and people were slain in the Spirit.) This was the fulfillment of what God had planned for Ralph's ministry; he was moving in healing and deliverance. After that experience, he was used mightily of God in YWAM counseling schools in the northeast US and Canada. Ralph has gone home to the Lord, and his daughter, Carol Allen, told me later that this trip changed his life. She transcribed some of Ralph's remembrances.

Carol Allen, Ralph Knepper's daughter: Dad told me that the morning he left to go on the trip, he felt God's presence and knew that it was going to be an awesome time. He did not know what God would do but he knew that it was going to be good.

I helped him with the outline of all the places you had been, but I do know that you went to New Zealand. Dad was in Australia for the time you were in NZ. He had a great time ministering to different YWAM bases. I do not know all the places in Australia he went. I know that he knew the people that he prayed over and did not forget them. I know he was really excited about the anointing of the Spirit and the healings and deliverances that you both experienced.

One place he went he got there before you. It had a bunch of doctors who were expecting you. He told me about that. He had the meeting in your absence.

He was so thrilled with how the Spirit of God would come into a meeting and the two of you would pray for people. He said almost everyone would be slain in the Holy Spirit. Sometimes a person would need to deal with unforgiveness or bitterness or some other issue and you would have him help work through the issue.

I know that when Dad went to the place to pick up the suit the tailor took him into the back room to have him pray deliverance over his wife. Then the tailor gave the suit to Dad. Dad had a real authority when it came to deliverance.

There was a place with an upper room that he talked about. He had some very meaningful conversations with a lady there. He told me over and over about the ministry sessions. There is nothing like the glory and seeing people healed and set free. He talked about it a lot.

Dad thought very highly of you. He was very thankful for the time that he had with you on the trip, but also, he spoke very highly of Donna and her ability to counsel. I used to wish Arnold and I could come to Oklahoma and have you pray for us, after listening to Dad. I am so glad you were obedient in inviting him to come along. It was one of the highlights of his life. I remember that you and Dad talked of Malaysia, Penang, and Kuala Lumpur.

Don: During this trip while I was in Malaysia, I was wanting a batik shirt to use for ministry since they are so much cooler. The brothers in Malaysia asked me if I needed to do any shopping. I told them that I would like to find a batik shirt. They took me to a tailor where I ordered a beautiful, tailored batik shirt that was done just before I flew to Jakarta, Indonesia. I taught the second night of the crusade since Ralph had spoken the first night. The Lord laid on my heart to again share about curses. It was a powerful night where we prayed for hundreds of people and observed the Lord once again setting people free.

I will always remember that toward the end of the prayer line, a man came forward and said, "Dr. Tredway, do you know what is on your shirt." I told him no and asked what it was. He said, "You are wearing a shirt with Indonesian gods on it." I felt the conviction of the Holy Spirit. I prayed about it that night, and the Lord told me to destroy it. I argued saying that I paid a lot of money for it and could I give it to someone. Even as I argued with the Lord, I knew the answer. I burned the shirt. How the enemy tries to trap us. Instead of praying about buying the shirt, I impulsively bought it. The irony of what I was wearing when I preached God's Word on bondages! We are accountable for God's truths that we preach and share.

While I was in Indonesia, and because of my academic background, I was asked to share with the medical students at the University of Indonesia. What a privilege. I once again shared my testimony of how Jesus' healing had changed my life. Only the Lord can open doors like that. I was so fulfilled as I flew home to Kona.

CHAPTER 9

Second Road to *Damascus* Experience

John 14:8,9 Philip said to Him, "Lord, show us the Father, and it is enough for us." Jesus said to him, "Have I been so long with you, and yet you have not come to know Me, Philip? He who has seen Me has seen the Father; how can you say, 'Show us the Father'?"

After the meetings in Kuala Lumpur, Malaysia, Indonesia, and Australia, I returned home to Kona. I was exhausted but so excited in the Lord. One morning a few days after returning home, the Lord told me to take my Bible and to go sit on the seawall in downtown Kona. As I sat there, He told me to open my Bible to Jude.

Jude 1:1 Jude, a bondservant of Jesus Christ, and brother of James, To those who are the called, beloved in God the Father, and kept for Jesus Christ:

"Beloved in God the Father" seemed to jump off the page to me. The Lord then instructed me to turn my Bible to **John 14.**

Verse 1 spoke to my heart, "Do not let your heart be troubled; believe in God, believe also in Me."

My heart was troubled that morning, and I had no understanding as to why after having such great victories in the Lord during my time in Malaysia, Indonesia, and Australia.

In answer to Thomas, Jesus says in John 14:6:

Verse 6, I am the way, and the truth, and the life; no one comes to the Father but through Me.

This is the basis of our faith in God through Jesus Christ. The word *Father* also jumped off the page to me as I read the rest of the chapter and noted that the word Father was mentioned twenty-three times.

Verse 21, "He who has My commandments and keeps them is the one who loves Me; and he who loves Me will be loved by My Father, and I will love him and will disclose Myself to him."

What are you saying God when you say, "I will disclose Myself to him"?

Verse 23 If anyone loves Me, he will keep My word; and My Father will love him, and We will come to him and make Our abode with him.

Again, I was trying to understand just what God was trying to say through "I will love him," just as I was trying to understand what He meant through "beloved in God the Father" in the passage in

Jude. In the following verses, I also noticed multiple references to the Holy Spirit.

> **Verse 26 and 27** "But the Helper, the Holy Spirit, whom the Father will send in My name, He will teach you all things, and bring to your remembrance all that I said to you. Peace I leave with you; My peace I give to you; not as the world gives do I give to you. Do not let your heart be troubled, nor let it be fearful."

My heart was perplexed, and I asked, "What are You trying to say to me after moving in my life the way You have?" Then He brought to my mind something that had happened after my graduation from the University of Southern California. It was a painful memory that I had buried deep. The Navy had sent me to obtain a PhD degree in Physiology while I did a Reproductive Endocrinology and Infertility Fellowship subspecialty training in Obstetrics and Gynecology. My father and mother, along with my elderly grandparents who had never been out of the Midwest or seen an ocean, came to see me graduate. I was the first grandchild to graduate from college, let alone to become a physician and to receive an academic PhD degree. We had an exciting time as a family (three generations) going to Knox Berry Farm, Disney Land in Anaheim, and seeing all the tourist sites. My mom, dad, and grandparents were so proud as I accepted my diploma dressed in my Dress White Navy Uniform, metals and all, on 6 June 1974.

The day before my family was to return home, my dad was tired and not feeling well. I checked him over. His BP was a little elevated but everything else seemed fine. He had just had his annual physical before coming to visit and everything was normal. He was tired and just wanted to go home.

We had a good night's rest and got up the next morning for the forty-five-minute drive to the airport. Just as I pulled out of the driveway of our home, my father, age 52, collapsed in the front seat next to me with my mother and grandparents in the back seat. I drove back into the driveway, stopped the car, and pulled my father out onto the driveway while Donna took the children, my mother, and grandparents into the house and called 911. I checked my father. He was pale, and I could not feel a pulse. I started an external cardiac massage, stopping to breathe for him. He vomited; I cleaned his airway and continued to resuscitate him. After several minutes, the paramedics arrived, intubated him to establish an airway, started an IV, and continued the external cardiac massage. They put him in an ambulance and wanted me to follow in a car. I refused and traveled with them in the ambulance. This was a father who had sacrificed for me so I could go to school, and I was not going to leave his side. I was using all my education to keep my father alive.

Donna had a neighbor watch the children while she brought my mother and grandparents to the nearby hospital in Cerritos. We arrived in the ER of the hospital, put him on a cardiac monitor, and he was in ventricular tachycardia (irregular heartbeat). He was given the appropriate IV medications and external cardiac shock three times. The first two times, the monitor was unchanged, but after the third shock, the cardiogram became a straight line. My father at age 52 on June 6, 1974, died in front of my eyes. I wanted to cry but I couldn't. As a physician, I was taught to be objective and not to get personally involved. Also, I was of English heritage, and we Tredways never showed our emotions. We kept it all inside. I never will forget that day. I wanted to cry and say, "Dad, I love you." I had never told my dad that I loved him, and he never said that he loved me. While wanting to cry but unable to, I had to go out and tell my mother that her husband had died and my grandparents that their son had died. They cried but I could not. I then had to sign my dad's death certificate, go to the airlines to change the tickets, make arrangements to fly my father's body home, and coordinate arrangements with a funeral home in Los Angeles with a local one in southern Illinois. I then flew home with my mother and grandparents. It was all a blur in my memory. I was an only child, so I had to be strong. It was an awful experience, and I had recurring nightmares for many months after that.

That day on the seawall as I read **Jude 1** and **John 14**, the Lord brought that memory back to my mind. He also showed me that the thing that pleased my father the most was how I did in school. That was how I felt my father's love. That is conditional love based upon performance, and that is how I felt about God. My earthly father was supposed to represent God the Father. How I saw God was dependent upon my earthly father's characteristics. I know my father loved me, but he was just like his father and his father before him. Love and acceptance for me was based upon performance, and that is how I saw God the Father.[21-23]

I had a flashback of ministry times. If no miracles or dramatic healing occurred at a service, I would ask God where I had failed Him. It even affected my relationship with Donna and my children. I couldn't believe they loved me unless I did or bought things for them. I did not understand unconditional love. **No wonder I did not feel "beloved in God the Father and kept for Jesus Christ."** I broke that day and cried as I never could before even at the death of my earthly father. That day the Lord showed me that despite seeing mighty miracles, the clinically dead raised, and all the signs and wonders, I didn't really know Him and His love. I did not understand that my acceptance by God was not based on performance and that I was loved unconditionally.

That day on the seawall I forgave my father for not being the father that God intended him to be. It wasn't his fault, just a characteristic handed down in the family. Even though I had had ministry of the Father-heart of God before, **I felt His love that day as never before. His love filled my soul, and there was no doubt in my mind that Don Tredway was beloved in God the Father and kept for Jesus Christ and that He is always with me. With that, I felt a security and peace in Him that I never had experienced before.** Even though I had been moving in the power of God, seeing physical and inner healings, people being set free from demonic forces, and even the raising of the clinically dead, I did not really know Him. Even though I did not know Him, God still used me. I had been moving out of works and performance. With the security of His love, He would later release me into greater works for His glory. It is so important to know and understand God's unconditional love. Once again, I return to one of the prime words of God in my life.

> **Philippians 3:14,15** I press on toward the goal for the prize of the upward call of God in Christ Jesus. Let us therefore, as many as are perfect, have this attitude; and if in anything you have a different attitude, God will reveal that also to you.

God revealed my wrong attitude toward Him that day. I am so loved by God that He allowed me to minister in His name even when I did not understand His unconditional love. He tells us that if we continue to press into Him and are obedient, He will reveal any misconceptions that we have of Him and heal us. What a loving Father we have. His love brings acceptance, security, and confidence of who we are in Him.[24]

Do you believe that you are unconditionally loved by God the Father, or are you like I was, believing that love is achieved through performance (works)? If that is you, please pray and ask the Holy Spirit to recall what it is that is blocking your relationship with the Father. Then move in forgiveness or do whatever He tells you to do so that you will come to know Him more deeply. He will be faithful! God showed me that day the importance of His commandment to "honor your father and mother."

> **Exodus 20:12** Honor your father and your mother, that your days may be prolonged in the land which the Lord your God gives you.

We must forgive our parents for not being the father or mother that God intended them to be. What a freeing revelation it was to know that I am loved unconditionally. The prodigal son returned home that day. I now have a deeper understanding of the significance of Matthew 6:14.

> **Matthew 6:14** For if you forgive others for their transgressions, your heavenly Father will also forgive you. But if you do not forgive others, then your Father will not forgive your transgressions.

It was during this time that someone recommended Henri Nouwen's book about the prodigal son.[25] This book has had a profound effect upon me, and I believe that the Holy Spirit would speak to you through this in-depth study. It, along with Rembrandt's painting of the Prodigal Son, has helped me to see where at various times in my life I identify with different characters in Rembrandt's painting. I have a copy of this painting hanging in my office reminding me every day of God's faithfulness and love.

While I praise God for my physical healing when I was in the Navy, which I call my first "road to Damascus experience," that day on the seawall when God revealed His love to me was truly my second "road to Damascus experience." The security that I feel in Him has allowed me to go through tremendous trials since then, and His love gives me a security that is hard to explain. It also has given me the confidence to know that He is with me during ministry time, which releases tremendous authority. I do not have to perform to be loved by Him; through Jesus Christ I am loved. Out of that love and relationship with the Father, ministry and authority in Him will flow.

Do you need to know the love of the Father? He is waiting for Jude 1 and John 14 to be fulfilled in your life. Call upon Him now for revelation in your life. I encourage you to spend time meditating on Appendix A.

Thank you for joining Donna and me on this first part of our journey with the Lord. Our story will continue from when I returned to full-time practice of medicine and the Lord took us from full-time ministry with YWAM into a marketplace ministry. I believe the Holy Spirit wanted us to end at this point to emphasize His unconditional love which is available to you also.

The revelation of God's love will change your life. Once you have that security and authority, along with increased compassion and love, it will be manifest in your ministry. With that increase, however, also comes a warning. The enemy will continually tempt you with pride. God will not share His glory.

Each one of us experiences trials of various degrees. God's love surrounds us during those times, but so often we do not recognize His love because of past experiences. God uses these trials to further His purpose in our life. Experiencing the love and acceptance of our heavenly Father is life-changing. I now understand Paul in Romans 8:38,39.

> **Romans 8:38,39** For I am convinced that neither death, nor life, nor angels, nor principalities, nor things present, nor things to come, nor powers, nor height, nor depth, nor any other created thing, will be able to separate us from the love of God, which is in Christ Jesus our Lord.

How long had I been used of Him but really did not know the depth of His love and His protective wall of love around me? **Is that you also? Seek Him today!**

> **2 Thessalonians 3:5** May the Lord direct your hearts into the love of God and into the steadfastness of Christ.

> **2 Timothy 1:7** For God has not given us a spirit of timidity, but of power and love and discipline.

Are you experiencing an emptiness in your life? If you do not know Jesus Christ and have not begun a walk with Him, would you pray now and ask Him to forgive you of your sins and ask Him to come into your life? He will fill that emptiness with His unconditional love and will introduce you to God the Father and the Holy Spirit.

> **John 14:6** Jesus *said to him, "I am the way, and the truth, and the life; no one comes to the Father but through Me."

> **Acts 2:21** And it shall be that everyone who calls on the name of the Lord will be saved.

Romans 10:9 that if you confess with your mouth Jesus as Lord and believe in your heart that God raised Him from the dead, you will be saved.

As you come into a new relationship with the character of God, just as you have come to know Jesus as a friend, come to know that you are beloved in God the Father, and let Him introduce you and fill you with the Holy Spirit. Come to know the Holy Spirit as the third person of the Trinity who will walk and talk with you. He will guide you through your path following the anointing of God just as He has guided Donna and myself in our journey. **The three persons of the Trinity await a new relationship with you!**

We hope that you have enjoyed the first part of our journey as we learned to follow the Lord and His Holy Spirit. It was very fulfilling as He led me from the practice of medicine to full-time ministry. I thought I had left medicine forever. As I became more secure in Him, based upon His love and acceptance, He had me return to medicine and a marketplace ministry. I would find different challenges and struggles as I tried to balance medicine, ministry, and family. Our journey continues in part two of "Following the Anointing, Marketplace Ministry."

Don and Donna at 2023 Aloha Ohana YWAM Korean Camp, Kona, Hawaii.

Appendices

The following appendices that were referred to in the above reading relate to teachings that the Lord released to us on the mission field. Often during devotion time or as I was praying about a service, the Lord would bring various scriptures to mind. Then as I would meditate on them, a teaching or message would come. Other times, the Lord would only give me one scripture to start with, and then as I spoke, He would bring various incidents in my life to mind along with other scripture. Let the Holy Spirit minister to you as He has to others. Thank you for joining us in our walk with the Lord.

APPENDIX A
CHARACTER OF GOD[9,21-32]

In this story of following God's anointing, I have placed what I consider the most important appendix first. As I noted in the last section concerning my second "Road to Damascus Experience," the truths that follow have been the keys to my growth and increasing anointing in God. As you will note, on multiple occasions I quoted that my goal in following God's anointing was best said by the apostle Paul in

> **Philippians 3:14,15** I press on toward the goal for the prize of the upward call of God in Christ Jesus. Let us therefore, as many as are perfect, have this attitude; and if in anything you have a different attitude, God will reveal that also to you.

The cry of my heart has been that as I trust in the Lord and press into Him, He will reveal any deficiencies or misconceptions that I have of Him. **The more I know Him, the more I can be used of Him.** His revelations come as I continue to press in and grow in His Word and experience His healing touch. The more I know Him, the more that I comprehend the depth and width of His love. There is more security and power of God residing in my life because of that love. People often ask how one can know God's power; the simple answer is, to know Him. The moto of YWAM is to "Know God and to Make Him Known." As you begin your walk with the Lord and follow His anointing, He will give you revelation of who He is!

The following appendix is but an introduction to the subject of "How Do You See God?"

SO, WHAT IS YOUR IMAGE OF GOD?

As we walk out Philippians 3:14,15 and press into Jesus with the understanding that we have in Him after accepting Him as Lord of our life, the following promises will become evident as we press into Him:

> **2 Corinthians 5:17** Therefore if any man is in Christ, he is a new creature; the old things passed away; behold, new things have come.

1 Thessalonians 5:23 Now may the peace of God Himself sanctify you entirely and may your spirit and soul and body be preserved complete, without blame at the coming of the Lord Jesus Christ.

1 John 1:9 If we confess our sins, He is faithful and righteous to forgive us our sins and to cleanse us from all unrighteousness.

That day on the seawall (Chapter 9) as I read Jude 1 about being beloved in **God the Father** and John 14 where the word *Father* was used twenty-three times, the Holy Spirit revealed to me that I did not really know Him. He took me back through situations in my life and showed me where I saw Him through the image of my earthly father. My father was a good father, but he was just like his father before him and like fathers of former generations. My love from my earthly father was based upon performance instead of unconditional love. Here I had been used of God, had seen His supernatural power, but I did not know Him. I remembered often reading the scriptures when Jesus asked Peter three times if he loved Him (**John 21:15-17**). I could feel Peter's anguish, for it was mine also. Then the following scripture gave me revelation:

John 14:28 You heard that I said to you, "I go away, and I will come to you." If you loved Me, you would have rejoiced because I go to the Father, for **the Father is greater than I** (emphasis mine).

As I forgave my father for not being the father that God intended him to be, Jesus took me home to the Father that day and I felt love as I never had before. Once I felt that love, my love for God filled my heart. Expressions of His love began to flow in ministry. I believe that this revelation was one of the major reasons God took me to YWAM.

How do you see God the Father? Is He an angry God pointing His finger at you, an alcoholic God, a worrying God, a scornful God, a judgmental God, a God not really involved with you, a workaholic God who was never home or was absent? Adam was created in the image of God and was to represent God to his children. So also, our earthly fathers represent God. As we accept the saving grace of Jesus Christ and come to the Father, old hurts/experiences from the past can cloud our concept of God. Consequently, we often see Him as an image of our earthly fathers or those who played that role in our lives. We need to be healed of these old hurts/experiences so that revelations of the true character of God can occur. That is what God in His Word is promising us.

For a more in-depth discussion and study of the different personality types and attributes that can be attributed to God's father image that are based upon our experiences in life, I would recommend Jack Frost's material on "Experiencing Father's Embrace."[21,22] Meditate upon these scriptures.

> **1 Corinthians 4:15** For if you were to have countless tutors in Christ, yet you would not have many fathers; for in Christ Jesus, I became your father through the Gospel.

> **John 10:30** I and the Father are one.

> **Hebrews 1:5** I will be a Father to Him, and He shall be a son to me.

> **John 14:6** I will not leave you as orphans.

> **Psalms 27:10** For my father and my mother have forsaken me,
> But the LORD will take me up.

> **Malachi 4:6 (AMP)** He will turn the hearts of the fathers to their children, and the hearts of the children to their fathers [a reconciliation

produced by repentance], so that I will not come and strike the land with a curse [of complete destruction].

These are God's promises to you now. I invite you to forgive your father if God has revealed to you any misconceptions that you may have of Him because your father (or others who fulfilled that role in your life) was not the father God intended him to be. As you do that, you will have better understanding of the following scripture:

Matthew 22:37-40 "YOU SHALL LOVE THE LORD YOUR GOD WITH ALL YOUR HEART, AND WITH ALL YOUR SOUL, AND WITH ALL YOUR MIND." This is the great and foremost commandment. The second is like it, "YOU SHALL LOVE YOUR NEIGHBOR AS YOURSELF." On these two commandments depend the whole Law and the Prophets.

Knowing that I am loved allows me to love others like I have never been able to love them before—part of the process of becoming that new creature in Christ. But in my journey of being loved and loving others, God began to show me more of His character. One day as I was meditating on the fulfillment of 2 Corinthians 6:17,18 (therefore, "COME OUT FROM THEIR MIDST AND BE SEPARATE," says the Lord. "AND DO NOT TOUCH WHAT IS UNCLEAN; and I will welcome you. And I will be a father to you, and you shall be sons and daughters to Me," says the Lord Almighty), the Holy Spirit had me read the following scripture.

2 Corinthians 7:1,2 Therefore, having these promises, beloved, let us cleanse ourselves from all defilement of flesh and spirit, perfecting holiness in the fear of God. **Make room for us in your hearts;** we wronged no one, we corrupted no one, we took advantage of no one (emphasis mine).

Make room for us in your hearts seemed to jump off the page. God, what are you saying? Then the HS reminded me of the Trinity. Jesus the Friend who took us home to the Father and the Holy Spirit, the Comforter. It is a composite of all three or an intersection of the three that comprise the character of God as shown in this diagram.

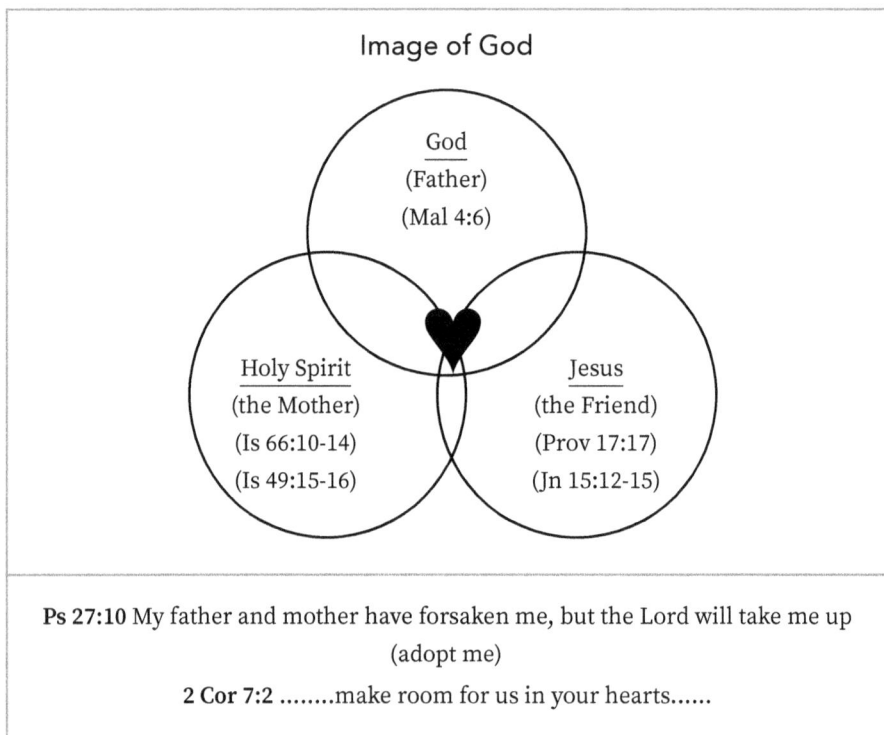

Image of God

God
‾‾‾‾
(Father)
(Mal 4:6)

Holy Spirit
‾‾‾‾‾‾‾‾‾‾
(the Mother)
(Is 66:10-14)
(Is 49:15-16)

Jesus
‾‾‾‾‾
(the Friend)
(Prov 17:17)
(Jn 15:12-15)

Ps 27:10 My father and mother have forsaken me, but the Lord will take me up (adopt me)

2 Cor 7:2 ....make room for us in your hearts......

How do you see **Jesus the Friend?**[33] Life experiences can also impact the way we view Jesus. Just as our earthly father influences the way we see the heavenly Father, our relationship with others, particularly our friends, can affect how Jesus is seen in our relationship with Him. Has there been a dominating, controlling friend, or one who ridiculed you? Perhaps there has been no friend or maybe there was someone who you thought was a friend but rejected or hurt you. If there have been such relationships, how can one really come to know and trust Jesus as a friend? Just as with that of the Father, one must choose to forgive. Ask the Holy Spirit to reveal those who have hurt you, to heal that part of your life and to reveal Jesus as the true and perfect Friend.

> **Proverbs 17:17** A friend loves all the time.

> **Proverbs 18:24** A man of many friends comes to ruin, but there is a friend who sticks closer than a brother.

> **John 15:12-15** This is My commandment, that you love one another, just as I have loved you. Greater love has no one than this, that one lay down his life for his friends. You are My friends if you do what I command you.

For a more in-depth discussion and study of different personality types and how they may affect how Jesus is seen, as well as the attributes that can be attributed to Jesus as a friend, do a more thorough study on "Jesus the Friend."[32,33]

The same principle also applies to that of the Holy Spirit, the **maternal side of God's character.**

The relationship with our mothers can also affect how we see the Holy Spirit. When you think of mother, what image comes to mind? Was she an angry mother, an alcoholic, depressed mother, one that always belittled you so that you could never please her, or was she absent from your life?

How can I be comforted until I know this part of God's character? Just as with the other deficiencies in our life regarding God the Father and Jesus the Friend, God will restore this maternal part of His character in our life as we forgive the failures of our earthly mother and ask the Lord to heal those deficiencies. If that is you, consider these promises from God's Word.

John 14:18 I will not leave you as orphans.

Jeremiah 31:3; 1:5 I have loved you with an everlasting love; therefore I have drawn you with loving kindness.... Before I formed you in the womb I knew you, and before you were born I consecrated you.

Ps 139:13,17-18; 71:6 For Thou didst form my inward part; Thou didst weave me in my mother's womb...How precious also are Thy thoughts to me, O God! How vast is the sum of them! If I should count then, they would outnumber the sand...By Thee I have been sustained from my birth; Thou art He who took me from my mother's womb; my praise is continually of Thee.

You have never been alone! You are not an accident!

Psalm 27:10; 68:5-6 My father and mother have forsaken me, but the Lord will take me up (adopt me as a child)...A father of the fatherless...God make a home for the lonely.

Isaiah 49:15-16 Can a woman forget her nursing child, and have no compassion on the son of her womb? Even these may forget, but I will not forget you. Behold, I have inscribed you on the palms of My hands.

Is 66:11-13 "That you may nurse and be satisfied with her comforting breast, that you may suck and be delighted with her bountiful bosom." For thus says the Lord, "Behold, I extend peace to her like a river, and the glory of the nations like an overflowing stream; and you shall be nursed, you shall be carried on the hip and fondled on the knees. As one whom his mother comforts, so I will comfort you; and you shall be comforted in Jerusalem."

Scripture confirms that **GOD WANTS TO COMFORT YOU IN HIS LOVE** so that you can show His comfort to others.

> **2 Corinthians 1:3-4** Blessed be the God and Father of our Lord Jesus Christ, the Father of mercies and God of all comfort, who comforts us in all our affliction so that we may be able to comfort those who are in any affliction with the comfort with which we ourselves are comforted by God.

For a more in-depth discussion and study of the maternal aspect of God's character, I recommend the following resources: Jack Frost's material, Experiencing Father's Embrace;[21,22] Wm Paul Young,[34,35] introduces the mother heart of God concept; Trudy Beyak's book, *The Mother Heart of God*;[36] and Diane Littleton's book, *The Nurturing God*[37] both discuss this concept in depth.

To know God in His fullness is to know the Trinity: God the Father, Jesus the Friend, and the Holy Spirit, His maternal character. As we look at the image of the three circles representing the Trinity, the character of God, I believe where the three intersect in the middle is where God wants us to be. I now understand our charge in

> **Matthew 28:18-20** All authority has been given to Me in heaven and on earth. Go therefore and make disciples of all the nations, baptizing them in the **name of the Father and the Son and the Holy Spirit,** teaching them to observe all that I commanded you; and lo, I am with you always, even to the end of the age (emphasis is mine).

How can one fully go forth in the name of the Father, the Son, and the Holy Spirit until he has dealt with deficiencies, resulting from life experiences, that blind one from knowing the true character of God? Thank you for walking with us as we followed and continue to follow His anointing in our lives. He invites you to

walk with Him today as never before. Will you say yes to His calling on your life? I encourage you to explore more your understanding of the character of God by referring to the references cited at the beginning of this chapter.

APPENDIX B
CHAPTER: MINISTRY OF JESUS[38-42]

When I was traveling with Dean Sherman in Australia and witnessing the power of God confirming His Word with signs and wonders, God began to speak to me about doing an in-depth study of the ministry of Jesus. Out of that study came this teaching that I have used in multiple YWAM schools and in part for various seminars.

IS JESUS WILLING TO HEAL?

The question is often asked, "Is God willing to heal?" Man (body, soul, and spirit) was once in direct relationship with God. However, as original sin was manifest, our relationship was displaced. Through generations of sin, we have become bruised in our body, soul, and spirit. God sent Jesus to bring us back into fellowship with Him. With Jesus' departure, the Holy Spirit was sent to indwell believers in order to bring forth healing and to move through them to continue His ministry. The following scripture answers the question, "Is God willing to heal?

> Luke 5:12,13 And it came about that while He was in one of the cities, behold, there was a man full of leprosy; and when he saw Jesus, he fell on his face and implored Him, saying, "Lord if You are willing, You can make me clean." And He stretched out His hand and touched him, saying, "I am willing; be cleansed."

GOD IS A GOOD GOD

Genesis1:1-31 And God saw all He had made and behold, it was very good.

Psalm 31:19 How great is Your goodness, which You have stored up for those who fear You, which You have wrought for those who take refuge in You, before the sons of men!

Psalm 145:9 The LORD is good to all, and His mercies are over all His works.

If God is a good God, then **what is sickness and disease and what are the causes?**

Let us again look at the scriptures noted below. There was no sickness or disease until the original sin of Adam noted in Genesis 3 and the fall from grace. Upon this original sin, then all living things that had life up until that time of original sin were to be governed by man. We have the sins of our forefathers (generational sins) noted in Deuteronomy 28 and then the actual sins that you and I do of our own free will. Often these layers are intertwined in a spiderweb of the enemy's handiwork. So what causes disease?

What Causes Disease?

1. Original, Generational, and Actual Sin

Genesis 3: fall from grace.

Deuteronomy 28:46 And they shall become a sign and a wonder on you and your descendants forever.

Deuteronomy 28 deals with the blessings of the Lord that result from following His laws and covenants. The remainder of the chapter lists the results of sin and disobedience.

Deuteronomy 28: 21,22 The Lord will make the pestilence cling to you until he has consumed you from the land where you are entering to possess it. The Lord will smite you with conception and with fever and with inflammation and with fiery heat and with the sword and with blight and with mildew, and they will pursue you until you perish.

From the Hebrew, Strong's dictionary defines pestilence as a plague. Fever, inflammation, heat, blight, and mildew are the same in Hebrew. This disease appears after the sin of disobedience. Later in verse 46 we see the effect on descendants. Deuteronomy 28:46 "And they shall become a sign and a wonder on you and your descendants forever."

The appearance of disease because of sins and disobedience is emphasized again later in this chapter.

Deuteronomy 28:58-61. If you are not careful to observe all the words of this law which are written in this book, to fear this honored and awesome name, the Lord your God, then the Lord will bring extraordinary plagues on you and your descendants, even severe and lasting plagues, and miserable and chronic sicknesses. He will bring back on you all the diseases of Egypt of which you were afraid, and they will cling to you. Also, every sickness and every plague which, not written in the book of this law, the Lord will bring on you until you are destroyed.

That gives us more understanding when Jesus says your sins are forgiven.

Matthew 9:2 Jesus said to the paralytic, "Take courage your sins are forgiven."

2. **Germs: Importance of Levitical laws to avoid that which is unclean.**

   We know that bacteria, viruses, parasites, and organisms that were no longer under control after original sin play havoc in the form of germs. Thus, the second cause of disease; germs. That is why the children of Israel were given the Levitical laws in order to avoid that which was unclean.

3. **Abuse of our Body: 1 Corinthians 6:19 ...your body is a temple of the Holy Spirit.**

   It is easy to blame other people or other things for our physical condition, but how often do we just abuse our bodies? Scripture tells us that a believer's body is the temple of God, but we often do not take care of it.

4. **Satan/Demons: Luke 13:11-13** Woman healed who was bent double by a sickness caused by a spirit. This cause was one that was hard for me to accept until I began to look through the eyes of the Holy Spirit. It exists today just as it did in the days of the Bible.

It is one thing to diagnose the cause of a disease, but what does Scripture say about healing? How does God heal?

PRINCIPLES OF HEALING: HOW GOD HEALS

1. **Sovereign Supernatural Acts of God:** Present in the Ministry of Jesus, Disciples, and Apostles

   Matthew 15:30-31 And great multitudes came to Him, bringing with them those who were lame, crippled, blind, dumb, and many others and they laid them down at His feet; and He healed them, so that the multitude marveled as they saw the dumb speaking, the crippled restored, and the lame walking, and the blind seeing: and they glorified the God of Israel.

2. **By Means:** He uses medicines and ointments.

   Luke 10:30-37 Parable of the good Samaritan

   Ezekiel 47:12 Leaves for healing

   2 Kings 20:7 Cake of figs upon the boil

3. **Physical Healing: Matthew 15:30-31** And great multitudes came to Him, bringing with them those who were lame, crippled, blind, dumb, and many others and they laid them down at His feet; and He healed them, so that the multitude marveled as they saw the dumb speaking, the crippled restored, and the lame walking, and the blind seeing: and they glorified the God of Israel.

Let us now take a closer look at the ministry of Jesus to see if we can learn from the principles of Jesus' ministry as shown in Scripture. Why did Jesus make a point of healing on the Sabbath as noted in the following scriptures?

Demoniac healed **Mark 1:21-28**

Withered hand healed **Luke 6:5-11**

Woman bent double **Luke 13:10-13** (not limited by man)

I believe Jesus made a point of healing on the Sabbath to emphasize that **He is not limited when He will release healing.**

The next common question that needs to be addressed is, **"What activates healing?"** Let us look at the woman with the issue of blood in **Mark 5:24-34.**

Mark 5:27 She heard of Jesus.

Mark 4:23 (AMP) If any man has ears to hear, let him be listening, (and perceive and comprehend.)

Mark 5:27 She came.

Mark 5:27 She overcame the crowd (hindrances)

Mark 5:28 She touched His garment (in faith believing that "If I touch His garments, I shall get well.")

Mark 5:33 She told what happened. ".... fell down before Him and told Him the whole truth." She gave God the glory.

Mark 5:34 "Daughter, your faith has made you well..."

We can learn from the sequence of events in this passage. She first heard about Jesus, then sought Him. She faced hindrances, as do we when seeking Jesus, but she overcame. Without being acknowledged she reached out and touched Him (His garment) in faith and was healed. The woman confessed feeling the healing power of the Holy Spirit and when challenged told what happened and gave glory to God. After the actions on her part, Jesus then acknowledged that her faith was the key to her healing. We can learn from this sequence of events as we seek healing from the Lord Jesus Christ.

Again, we see the important of seeking Jesus through the story of the ten lepers.

Luke 17:11-19 and the ten lepers raised their voices, saying "Jesus, Master, have mercy on us."

:14 "Go and show yourself to the priests. And it came about that as they were going, they were cleansed."

:17 only one returned giving thanks to Him (a Samaritan).

:19 And Jesus said to him, "Rise, and go your way; your faith has made you well."

The same type of sequence of events as in the story of the woman with the issue of blood, but in addition, an instruction was given. Since they had been labeled by the priest as being unclean because of leprosy **(Leviticus 13:44)**, they had to return to the priest for confirmation of healing to fulfill the laws concerning leprosy **(Leviticus 14)**. Notice they were healed as they went back to the priest. I cannot help but think how many people had been in the presence of God seeking healing but did not go back to their physician for confirmation. We all want a sudden dramatic healing, but often it is gradual, being confirmed by the physician. What a witness it is to a physician when he witnesses a healing that he cannot explain except through the works of the Holy Spirit. It is interesting to note that only a foreigner (the Samaritan, not a believer of the Law) returned to Jesus. Again, Jesus acknowledged his faith.

METHODS OF HEALING

Let us now look at the methods by which Jesus released healing into people's lives. Just as for the disciples, Jesus is our example, and we are to imitate Him.

To Touch Jesus

We have seen how the woman with the issue of blood reached out in faith and touched Jesus **(Mark 5:21-43)**. Note the other scriptures in alignment with this principle.

Mark 5:21-43 woman with the issue of blood

Matthew 14:36 ...and they began to entreat Him that they might just touch the fringe of His cloak; and as many as touched it were cured.

Luke 6:19 And all the multitude were trying to touch Him, for power was coming from Him and healing them all.

There have been times during ministry when the anointing was so strong that the same type of anointing was present. As people reached out and touched my clothing or person, they were healed. It was not me they had to see, but Jesus in me. **Do people see Jesus in you? The Holy Spirit wants that relationship with you.**

Jesus' Touch (LAYING ON OF HANDS)

If Jesus is in us, then there will be times that He will have us touch others in order for them to be healed as noted in the following scriptures:

Matthew 8:3 He stretched out His hand and touched him (healing the leper).

Matthew 8:15 But when Jesus touched her hand, the fever left her. (Peter's mother-in-law)

We have witnessed this type of ministry in many evangelists such as Oral Roberts[41] and Kenneth Hagin.[42]

Words of Knowledge

Words of knowledge are important gifts of the Holy Spirit as noted in the following scriptures:

> **Luke 6:8** But He knew what they were thinking, and he said to the man with the withered hand, "rise and come forward." **:10** "stretch out your hand."

> **John 4:** the Samaritan woman at the well, word of knowledge about her husband

> **19:** Sir, I perceive that you are a prophet

> **Luke 4:22** (in Nazareth) Is this not Joseph's son?

> **:23** and He said to them, "No doubt you will quote this proverb to me, 'Physician heal yourself! Whatever we heard was done at Capernaum, do here in your home as well.'"

Words of knowledge will release faith in individuals. Also, note in Luke 4 that while in Nazareth, the people did not acknowledge Jesus as the Messiah but only as the son of Joseph. Again, people have to see Jesus in us not who we are in the world. I often heard Oral Roberts say on multiple occasions, "Only follow me as long as you see Jesus in me." What a profound statement. We should follow the Spirit of God in men not for who they are in the world.

Jesus' Command

Just as with Jesus, sometimes the Holy Spirit will release an action for someone to do just as Elijah told Naaman to go wash in the Jordan (**2 Kings 5:14-17**). Often, we are hesitant to go do what the

Holy Spirit directs as was Naaman. Hopefully we will have others around us to encourage us to do what the man of God directs.

> **Mark 2:10-11** He said to the paralytic, "I say to you, rise, take up your pallet and go home."

> **Mark 10:49-52** to the blind man "Go your way, your faith has made you well."

> **Luke 11:20** command by the finger of God

Notice the finger of God mention in **Luke 11**. Kathryn Kuhlman would often point into an audience and the Holy Spirit would come upon an individual. This has also happened in our ministry, as well as in other ministries, when the presence of God filled the room. You know it is the Holy Spirit and not a man when this occurs. We are to be only vessels of the Holy Spirit.

Praying at a Distance

> **Matthew 8:5-13** Centurion's servant healed from a distance.

How often have we seen people ask for prayer for a relative or someone who is not at a meeting and have seen God honor those prayers and heal, just as He did the centurion's servant.

In our time with YWAM, I have seen the power of intercessory prayer demonstrated. Also, as we move in the ministry of Jesus, praying for others through today's modern means of communication that reaches distant places, God moves and heals and will confirm His anointing.

Persistence

How often have I heard someone say, "Well I prayed once and that is enough." Yes, sometimes it is, yet if Jesus had to pray for the blind man more than once, then I may also have to pray more.

> **Mark 8:22-25** The blind man first saw shadows like trees, then clearly with more prayer.

Also recall the story of the friend at night wanting a loaf of bread and the widow before the judge. Persistence before God can and will bring healing.

> **Luke 11:5-10** Parable of the man wanting to borrow three loaves of bread at midnight for a friend who had just arrived for a visit and there was no bread to eat.

> **Luke 18:1-14** Parable of persistent widow before a judge wanting justice.

I cannot but question at times if we had been more persistent in prayer.

Different Means

This topic really challenged me, as I have shared with you regarding the move of God at Good News Church in Corona, California. God challenged me by asking me, **"Are you willing to be a fool for Me?"** With all my education, the Holy Spirit had me repeat each one of these scriptural examples during that move of God. His power was profound as people were touched and healed.

Mark 8:23 spit in blind eyes.

Mark 7:33-35 spit in ears.

John 9:6 mud and spit to eyes of blind, told to wash in pool of Siloam.

John 20:22 And he breathed on them and said, "Receive the HS."

Are you willing to be like Jesus and even be a fool in the sight of the world?

Confirmation

Mark 2:14 told the leper to go to priest.

As mentioned earlier, those who feel that they have been healed by the Lord should return to their doctor for confirmation. Sometimes healing is gradual. For instance, I have seen the need of insulin decrease over time and be confirmed as the individual returned to the physician. God will not be "put in a box" as to how or when He will heal. One must walk out their healing in the way He chooses.

Vulnerability

God really spoke to me through the following scripture.

Lk 22:50,51 the servant's ear at Gethsemane.

If you were a temple servant and had gone with the troops to arrest this man, Jesus, in the middle of the night and had one of His fanatical disciples whack your ear off with a sword, what would you think of Jesus? I don't think you would be very receptive to Him walking up to you. Jesus made Himself vulnerable as He went forward to that servant. I would like to know more about this servant after he was healed by Jesus. Yes, at times, we need to be willing to make ourselves vulnerable (put ourselves in danger) as we pray for healing in the name of Jesus. That is why it is important to make sure that we have a word of the Lord and are in His anointing as we minister.

Deliverance

Certain illness can be caused by demonic activity (as previously shared in the story of our friend Ellen who was paralyzed on one side of her body and blind in one eye).

Matthew 4:23,24 ...and they brought to Him all who were ill, taken with various diseases and pains, demoniacs, epileptics, paralytics, and He healed them.

Matthew 17:18 the boy with seizures. The demon came out when Jesus rebuked it and the boy was cured (physical illness and demons).

Only through moving in discernment (1 Corinthians 12:10—one of the gifts of the Holy Spirit) can we recognize when the enemy is involved. When moving in the power of God during such times, you may experience the indignation of the Lord when seeing His children bound by the works of the enemy.

The Awesome Presence of God

The ability of the power of the Holy Spirit to move in our lives is witnessed by observing scripturally how the Holy Spirit moved in the lives of the disciples and apostles in Scripture. Jesus promised the disciples that the Holy Spirit would come upon them, and we see impressive manifestations of the power and presence of God upon Peter and Paul as noted in the following scriptures.

Acts 5:15 Peter's shadow.

Acts 19:12 Paul's handkerchiefs, aprons.

Scripture tells us that healings were manifest from Peter's shadow and from Paul laying hands on handkerchiefs and aprons. Oral Roberts in his television ministry often talked about a point of contact where he would tell people to put their hands upon the TV as he prayed. Healings have also occurred from prayers that were prayed over objects and given to individuals. God is omnipresent and does amazing things. He is looking for servants to follow Jesus and to be used by Him.

WHAT ACTIVATES HEALING?

As we look at the multiple scriptures mentioned in the discussion above, we note the following attributes mentioned.

Faith: Faith seems to be in two categories in Scripture, that of ourselves and that of others.

Of Ourselves:

Mark 5:24-34 Woman with issue of blood

Luke 17:12-19 Ten lepers

Of Others:

Matthew 8:5-13 Centurion's servant

Matthew 9:18-26 royal official's daughter

But is faith all conclusive as some would have us believe? The following scriptures note that the faith of the individual is not associated with all healings.

Faith is not always involved:

John 9:38 Faith of blind man came after healing.

Matthew 9:18-26 Royal official's daughter was dead, and they laughed at Jesus.

Luke 7:12-17 Widow's dead son at a funeral.

Certainly, the dead son, the mother, and the members of the funeral procession did not have faith for the widow's son to be raised from the dead. Oh, what an event that must have been. Yes, faith is important, but there must be more.

If God is good, as we have discussed, then we also need to consider the faithfulness of God. He is faithful. It is His character as we will see in the scriptures below.

Faithfulness of God:

2 Timothy 2:13 If we are faithless, He remains faithful; for He cannot deny Himself.

Matthew 14:22-33 and Mark 6:45-52 Peter walking on water twice after He said "Lord save Me." Jesus took his hand and said to him, "O you of little faith, why did you doubt?"

I must admit that some of the most exceptional healings and moves of God that have occurred during times of ministry have happened when I had little or no faith. At the end of ministry times when I was exhausted and trying to leave, people would stop me wanting prayer. Often I would pray with the intention of getting it over with, and I would see God touch and heal people. He does it because that is His character. It is certainly Him and not me.

To try to get an understanding upon the importance of various factors such as an individual's faith, the faith of others, a sovereign act of God, and demonic factors, I looked at all the healings and works of Christ mentioned in the four Gospels. Using my scientific approach and evaluation, I tried to assign the importance of each factor mentioned in the Gospels. I found the various items were mentioned as noted below:

Study of All the Miracles of Jesus:

Faith 23%
　　Individual faith 67%
　　Others' faith 23%
Sovereign Act of God 40%
Demonic 30%
Sin 5%

More than one reason was mentioned in some of the healings, so I could not clearly assign them to an individual item. Consequently, one does not always end up with 100 percent. If you would go through and do the same exercise you might end up with a slightly different outcome, but I believe we would end up in the same ballpark. I was surprised that faith was only mentioned 23% of the time. When it was mentioned, individual faith was at 67% of the total faith category. Still, the importance of others' faith, such as the centurion's, and intercession was evident at 23% when faith was mentioned. Sovereign act of God was strongly evident 40% of the time because that is His character, a loving and good God that does good things even without faith being mentioned. The presence of the evil one, demonic causes of illness or maladies, is evident at 30%. If one denies this demonic source of illness, then you are denying almost one third of the ministry of Christ. I was surprised that sin was only mentioned 5% of the time. The Lord has used this analysis to keep me in balance. If I would concentrate in just one area, He would speak to me to come back into balance. We are to be imitators of Jesus Christ and His ministry.

Using that same approach, I then looked at the ministry of the apostles and found the following:

Apostles:

Faith 23%
Demonic 30%
Sovereign Acts of God 50%

Faith and the demonic were the same, but look at the sovereign acts of God. I cannot explain it except for His character. Let us look at an important scripture about Peter when the lame beggar was healed in order to get a little more insight into what activated the beggar's healing.

Acts 3: (AMP)

:16 and His name, through and by faith in His name, has made this man who you see and recognize well and strong. Yes, the faith which is through and by Him (Jesus) has given the man this perfect soundness (of body) before all of you.

:4 Look at us.

:7,8 and seizing him by the right hand, he raised him up; and immediately his feet and his ankles were strengthened. And with a leap, he stood upright and began to walk; and he entered the temple with them, walking and leaping and praising God.

Yes, Peter's faith of who he was in God released the glory of God. As we are secure in Him, as we are obedient to Him, as we are sensitive to the HS, as know we are beloved in Him, we will be powerful servants of God whose purpose is to take others into God's presence. It is God's promise that He will be with us.

Mark 16:15-20 (AMP) And He said to them, "Go into all the world and preach the gospel to all creation. He who has believed [in Me] and has been baptized will be saved [from the penalty of God's wrath and judgment]; but he who has not believed will be condemned. These signs will accompany those who have believed: in My name they will cast out demons, they will speak in new tongues; they will pick up serpents, and if they drink anything deadly, it will not hurt them; they will lay hands on the sick, and they will get well." So then, when the Lord Jesus had spoken to them, He was taken up into heaven and sat down at the right hand of God. And they went out and preached everywhere, **while the Lord was working with them and confirming the word by the signs that followed** (bold emphasis is mine).

Note the last sentence which is written in bold letters. As we do as we are commanded, the Lord will be with us confirming His Word with signs and wonders. Do you have that confidence that He is with you? Are you expecting Him to reveal Himself? Are you any different than Peter? Have you had times that you walked with Him, doubted Him, and perhaps even have denied what He has called you to do just as Peter did? He can change and use you just as He did Peter. Do you love me, Peter?

> **John 17:15-17 (AMP)** So when they had finished breakfast, Jesus said to Simon Peter, "Simon, son of John, do you love Me more than these [others do—with total commitment and devotion]?" He said to Him, "Yes, Lord; You know that I love You [with a deep, personal affection, as for a close friend]." Jesus said to him, "Feed My lambs." Again He said to him a second time, "Simon, son of John, do you love Me [with total commitment and devotion]?" He said to Him, "Yes, Lord; You know that I love You [with a deep, personal affection, as for a close friend]." Jesus said to him, "Shepherd My sheep." He said to him the third time, "Simon, son of John, do you love Me [with a deep, personal affection for Me, as for a close friend]?" Peter was grieved that He asked him the third time, "Do you [really] love Me [with a deep, personal affection, as for a close friend]?"And he said to Him, "Lord, You know everything; You know that I love You [with a deep, personal affection, as for a close friend]." Jesus said to him, "Feed My sheep.

After the resurrection, Jesus asked Peter three times if he loved Him, and He asks us the same question. For several years the Holy Spirit would take me to this exchange between Jesus and Peter, and I knew God was saying there was more to this scripture than I understood. When I finally had the revelation as to how much God loved me, along with the security and comfort that comes from that love (see the chapter on the Mother Heart of God), and that I did not have to strive to prove myself to Him, there came a confidence that I believe Peter had when he reached out his hand to the lame beggar in **Acts 3**.

Do you have that deep love for Him and know without a doubt that you are beloved in God the Father and kept for Jesus Christ (Jude 1:1)? Once you are at that place of knowing that love and the security that comes from that love, you can move in the faith just as Peter did. With the confidence of knowing who we are in the Lord, we are ready to be trained and released by the Holy Spirit in the various gifts of the Spirit. You may move in some gifts more often than others, but we are to be imitators of Christ, and the Holy Spirit will release you into whatever gift is necessary for that moment.

> **1 Corinthians 12:4 (AMP)** Now there are distinctive varieties and distributions of endowments [extraordinary powers distinguishing certain Christians, due to the power of divine grace operating in their souls by the Holy Spirit] and they vary, but the (Holy) Spirit remains the same.

> **9,10** to another (wonder –working) faith by the same (Holy) Spirit, to another the extraordinary powers of healing by the one Spirit, to another the working of miracles, to another prophetic insight—that is, the gift of interpreting the divine will and purpose; to another the ability to discern and distinguish between [the utterances of true] spirits and [false one], to another various kind of [unknown] tongues, to another the ability to interpret [such] tongues.

As Donna and I have related in our story of following His anointing, He will release you into the gifts you need for the appropriate occasions as needed. If you are open to Him, you will move in all these gifts as needed. Yes, you may move in some gifts more often, but we are to be imitators of Christ, and the HS will release you into what is necessary at the appropriate time.

In view of this understanding, let us examine again the Great Commission in The Message (MSG) version.

Mark 16:15-20 (MSG) Then He said to them, "Go into the world. Go everywhere and announce the Message of God's good news to one and all. Whoever believes and is baptized is saved; whoever refuses to believe is damned. These are some of the signs that will accompany believers: They will throw out demons in My name, they will speak in new tongues, they will take snakes in their hands, they will drink poison and not be hurt, they will lay hands on the sick and make them well." Then the Master Jesus, after briefing them, was taken up to heaven, and He sat down beside God in the place of honor. And the disciples went everywhere preaching, the Master working right with them, validating the Message with indisputable evidence.

My charge and yours is to take people into God's presence (power) where He does what is necessary (healing) for the individual.

PRINCIPLES OF INNER HEALING[43-47]

HURTS IMPOSED BY OTHERS

Job 17:1 My spirit is broken, my days are extinguished, the grave is ready for me.

Prov 15:13 A joyful heart makes a cheerful face, but when the heart is sad, the spirit is broken.

Prov 17: 22 A joyful heart is good medicine, but a broken spirit dries up the bones.

Prov 18:14 The spirit of a man can endure his sickness, but as for a broken spirit who can bear it?

Often during times of ministry, the Holy Spirit will give words of knowledge dealing with some misconception or hurt of the past that the individual experienced. The root cause of the hurt is brought to light by the Holy Spirit, and the individual is given the opportunity to deal with it. It may involve forgiveness or some kind of action on their part. If the individual is then willing, the Holy Spirit moves, gives revelation, and brings forth healing in that area. **God loves us so much that He sent His Son to walk along the paths of our lives to bring revelation, healing, and restoration.**

HURTS IMPOSED THROUGH ACTUAL SIN OF THE INDIVIDUAL

> **James 4:6-8** But He gives a greater grace, therefore it says, "God is opposed to the proud, but gives grace to the humble." Cleanse your hands, you sinners and purify your hearts, you double-minded.

This verse speaks to us about having impure hearts, not being humble, and being double-minded. The admonition is to be cleansed. In Ezekiel we are challenged to repent and turn away so that our sins do not become a stumbling block.

> **Ezekiel 18:30** Therefore I will judge you, O House of Israel, each according to his own conduct, declares the Lord God. Repent and turn away from all transgressions, so that your iniquity may not be a stumbling block to you.

Iniquity is described as a sin, depravity, or misery.

> **Jeremiah 8:10-11** ... From the prophet even to the priest everyone practices deceit, and they heal the brokenness of the daughter of my people superficially saying "Peace, peace but there is no peace."

> **Jeremiah 6:13-14** for from the least of them even to the greatest of them, everyone is greedy for gain, and from the prophet even to the priest, everyone deals falsely, and they heal the brokenness of My people superficially. Saying, "Peace, peace but there is no peace."

HOW HEALING COMES FOR INDIVIDUAL ACTUAL SINS

> **Revelation 12:11** the blood of the lamb. "And they overcame him because of the blood of the Lamb and because of the word of their testimony, and they did not love their life even to death."

Let us look at two righteous kings that brought the children of Israel back into relationship with God. King Hezekiah in **2 Chronicles 29** applied "the blood of the Lamb" to accomplish this restoring of relationship as did King Josiah **(2 Kings 23)**. But in addition to this, they had the people repent, consecrate themselves, and then apply the blood sacrifice. Are we forgetting to do the repenting and consecrating ourselves before we apply the blood sacrifice of Jesus Christ? If I have committed a sin, it must be confessed fulling the Scripture.

> **James 5:13-16 (AMP)** Confess to another therefore your faults—your slips, your false steps, your offenses, your sins; and pray (also) for one another, that you may be healed and restored—to a spiritual tone of mind and heart. The earnest (heartfelt, continued) prayer of a righteous man makes tremendous power available—dynamic in its working.

I am forgiven through the sacrifice of Jesus, but the Holy Spirit will bring to mind specific sins that need repenting of in order to bring about healing. With that act, the Holy Spirit is free to move in healing in those areas of my life.

> **2 Corinthians 5:17** Therefore if anyone is in Christ, he is a new creature; the old things passed away; behold, new things have come.

Satan attempts to block the Holy Spirit in the area of inner healing because he wants us crippled in order to diminish the workings of Christ through us. He has taken the notion of inner healing to extremes (false balances) by introducing concepts of mind healing cults, certain aspects of psychology and psychiatry, Sylvia mind control, etc. The enemy's tactic with any truth is to take it to a twisted extreme.

> **Proverbs 11:1 (AMP)** A false balance and unrighteous dealing are extremely offensive and shamefully sinful to the Lord, but a just weight is His delight.

In psychology and psychiatry, there are methods that help such as transference, biofeedback, and relaxation. While these techniques can help deal with life's tensions, they are powerless to deal with the soul's (inner man's) tensions. Often the inner conflicts are expressed physically. Relaxation techniques and transference to different areas of the body may help a person to function better; but to have a soul that is free of tension one needs to come to God to be healed.

> **Romans 12:2** Do not conform to the pattern of this world but be trans-formed by the renewing of your mind.

To emphasize this point, note The Message (MSG) translation of this verse.

> **Romans 12:2 (MSG)** Don't become so well-adjusted to your culture that you fit into it without even thinking. Instead, fix your attention on God. You'll be changed from the inside out.

Let us examine again the ministry of Jesus in Scripture from the perspective of inner healing.

Matthew 4:23-24 And Jesus was going about in all Galilee, teaching in the synagogues, and proclaiming the gospel of the kingdom, and healing every kind of disease and every kind of sickness among the people. And the news about Him went out into all Syria; and they brought to Him all who were ill, taken with various diseases and pains, epileptics, paralytics, and He healed them.

Let us expand upon the phrase "healing every kind of disease and every kind of sickness."

Matthew 5:4 Blessed are those who mourn, for they shall be comforted.

Matthew 23:25-28 Scribes and Pharisees: Clean the Inside of the Cup. "Woe to you, Scribes and Pharisees, hypocrites! For you clean the outside of the cup and of the dish, but inside they are full of robbery and self-indulgence. You blind Pharisee, first clean the inside of the cup and of the dish, so that the outside of it may become clean also. Woe to you, Scribes and Pharisees, hypocrites! For you are like whitewashed tombs which on the outside appear beautiful, but inside they are full of dead men's bones and all uncleanness. Even so you outwardly appear righteous to men, but inwardly you are full of hypocrisy and lawlessness."

Christ is speaking to what is on the inside of man, not what appears outwardly. Often what is apparent on the outside is only a symptom of what is on the inside.

Let's look at other scriptures that indicate the need for inner healing:

Proverbs 15:4 A soothing tongue is a tree of life, but perversion in it crushes the spirit.

Proverbs 15:13 A joyful heart makes a cheerful face, but when the heart is sad, the spirit is broken.

Proverbs 17:22 A joyful heart is good medicine, but a broken spirit dries up the bones.

Proverbs 18:14 The spirit of a man can endure his sickness but a broken spirit who can bear.

Psalms 131:2,3 Surely, I have composed and quieted my Soul... Like a weaned child rests against its mother, my soul is like a weaned child within me.

1 Corinthians 14:20 Brothers, stop being like children.

1 Corinthians 13:11 When I became a man, I put childish ways behind me.

Matthew 26:38 My soul is overwhelmed with sorrow to the point of death.

Psalms 22:7 All who see me mock me; they hurl insults, shaking their heads.

Psalms 69:3 I am worn out calling for help; my throat is parched.

Matthew 26:40 Could you men not keep watch with me for one hour.

Matthew 26:56 All the disciples deserted him and fled. (How do you think Christ felt?)

Hebrews 2:18 Because He himself suffered when He was tempted, He is able to help those who are being tempted.

And an important scripture for healing.

Hebrews 4:15 For we do not have a high priest who is unable to sympathize with our weakness, but we have one who has been tempted in every way, just as we are.

Christ was tempted and hurt in every way that we are but had victory over it all by enduring and not sinning. Healing, physical as well as emotional, is possible for us because of His victory.

If there is emotional trauma from an experience in life, healing is available as Jesus walks you back during those times, with Him at your side, to bring healing to the experience. Many times that healing involves forgiveness on the part of the person who was hurt.

By healing, the Lord can turn our hurts into advantages for Him. He will allow us to identify with others that have been hurt in similar ways in order to release the Holy Spirit into their lives to bring about their healing.

That is part of becoming a new creature in Christ. During times of ministry as the above scripture was being read, I have witnessed the Holy Spirit speaking into people's lives, healing and setting them free fulfilling the following scripture.

Hebrews 4:12-13 for the Word of God is living and active and sharper than any two-edged sword and piercing as far as the division of soul and spirit, of both joints and marrow, and able to judge the thoughts and intentions of the heart. And there is no creature hidden from His sight, but all things are open and laid bare to the eyes of Him with whom we have to do.

With this in mind, meditate and see what the Lord speaks to you by reading **Psalm 146** and **Isaiah 61**.

1 Thessalonians 5:23 Now may the peace of God Himself sanctify you entirely and may your spirit and soul and body be preserved complete, without blame at the coming of our Lord Jesus Christ.

The important point to remember is that NO MATTER WHAT PAIN YOU HAVE ENDURED—JESUS KNOWS AND UNDERSTANDS. HE HAS BEEN THROUGH IT ALL, AND HE CAN HEAL YOU!

Let us reexamine this scripture.

Philippians 3:14,15 I press on toward the goal for the prize of the upward call of God in Christ Jesus. Let us therefore, as many as are perfect, have this attitude; and if in anything you have a different attitude, God will reveal that also to you.

Notice what a promise of God that scripture is. If I continue to press into God and grow in His Word and understanding of His character, then at the appropriate time, if I have any attitude that is contrary to that, He will reveal it by His Spirit. Anything that He reveals He can heal as we move in repentance and forgiveness. Of course, it is my choice of whether to deal with those situations or not. When revelation comes by the HS, Scripture says:

1 Thessalonians 5:19 Do not quench the Spirit.

Matthew 11:28 Come to Me, all who are weary and heavy-laden, and I will give you rest.

Is your soul troubled? Has the HS revealed something on the inside to you? Do you need rest now? Call upon the name of the Lord!

PRINCIPLES OF INNER HEALING FOR SHAME

In this section we deal with the subject of shame. When ministering in Asia I became very aware of this powerful tool of the enemy and began to see this also reflected in Matthew 5.

> Matthew 5:3,4 Blessed are the poor in spirit, for theirs is the kingdom of heaven.
> Blessed are those who mourn, for they shall be comforted.

In Asia the term "losing face" (to become shameful) is used, and people go to great lengths to avoid it. We are all wounded. Situations in life happen. People hurt us and we hurt ourselves. Consequently, we mourn or grieve just the same as after a death of a loved one. Looking at this from an academic perspective, if I would make a mistake in a clinical trial, publish wrong results, and subsequently be proven wrong by another investigator, I could be put to shame, and it could affect my reputation. When I am faced with shame, I can choose to deal with it, deny it, or even try to cover it up.

A dear friend, Dr. Carol Peters-Tanksley, MD, DMin, a colleague of mine at Loma Linda University who will be introduced later in part II of our story, wrote in one of her daily meditations describing shame as an infected wound and gave an excellent teaching which I have slightly modified and reproduced with permission.[48,49] She notes that when the infection of shame sets in, the pain of those wounds can become unbearable and permanent. What are some examples? Wounds such as child abuse, domestic violence, mental illness, marital infidelity, business failure, abortion, or addiction are always painful. Why is it that some people seem to overcome them, heal from the wounds, and move on while others seem paralyzed (stuck) as though the wound happened just yesterday? Dr. Carol states that the difference is shame.

Psalm 69:19,20 You know my reproach and my shame and my dishonor; all my adversaries are before You. Reproach has broken my heart and I am so sick. And I looked for sympathy, but there was none, and for comforters, but I found none.

Using her analogy, shame is like an infection in a wound in which healing is not occurring. There are many sides to shame. We have just described individual shame but there is also corporate, cultural, and family (generational) shame. Dr. Carol has us look at the story of Ahab and the prophet of God Elijah.

1 Kings 18:20-21 So Ahab sent a message among all the sons of Israel and brought the prophets together at Mount Carmel. Elijah came near to all the people and said, "How long will you hesitate between two opinions? If the Lord is God, follow Him; but if Baal, follow him." But the people did not answer him a word.

Why did the people not answer the prophet? It is because of shame. Notice what Elijah said next to the people.

1 Kings 18:22-24 Then Elijah said to the people, "I alone am left a prophet of the Lord, but Baal's prophets are 450 men. Now let them give us two oxen; and let them choose one ox for themselves and cut it up, and place it on the wood, but put no fire under it; and I will prepare the other ox and lay it on the wood, and I will not put a fire under it. Then you call on the name of your god, and I will call on the name of the Lord, and the God who answers by fire, He is God." And all the people said, "That is a good idea.

The prophet gave them a way out, an offer they could not refuse, a way **to save face**—that is a way not to look so shameful for being silent. How often are we silent and shameful before God because of our family, our society, and our country.

Again, using infections as an analogy, Dr. Carol notes that healing doesn't happen once shame infects individual or family wounds unless the infection is addressed. Family (generational sins) are often the platforms that the enemy wants to build on in our lives. Both Dr. Carol and I as physicians know that sometimes we must treat a patient whose surgical wound has become infected. Those wounds are incredibly painful, and they won't heal until the infection is eliminated or the boil (abscess) is lanced. Shame is like that infection.

You'll only be healed from the wounds that others have caused you and that you've caused yourself when you bring your shame into the light of the Lord Jesus Christ. His light is like the scalpel that lances the abscess. Dr. Carol gives us an understanding of this light.

1. Light is a tremendous disinfectant.

2. Light kills bacteria. Sunlight kills most harmful bacteria wherever it's allowed to reach. High-intensity ultraviolet light will disinfect even the most resistant bacteria that have become established in a hospital environment.

3. Light eliminates darkness. Bacteria love warm dark places. You can't eliminate darkness by shoving it out, but turn on the light and darkness no longer exists. The abscess must be opened to the light!

4. Light heals. You perhaps know this best in the mental health arena. Seasonal affective disorder (SAD) happens during long winter months of increased darkness. Getting out in the sunlight is biochemically proven to make your brain work better and lift your mood.

That sounds good for bacteria, but what about shame? How do you bring it into the light?

The truth of His word is the disinfecting light that will eliminate shame, and the revelation of the truth by the Holy Spirit is the scalpel.

John 8:31,32 So Jesus was saying to those Jews who had believed Him, "If you continue in My word, then you are truly disciples of Mine; and you will know the truth, and the truth will make you free."

Dr. Carol notes three areas of truth that work together to heal and eliminate your shame.

1. **The truth about you.**

The picture of shame is that of hiding—from yourself, from others, and even from God.

Shining the light of truth on your shame means coming out of hiding. Be honest with yourself about what happened and about what you did or didn't do in response. Tell someone else who is safe about what happened. It's like draining the pus from an infected wound (lancing an abscess); it may hurt initially, but then healing can begin. Once you open your mouth you are also releasing the creative power of God (remember He spoke the world into being). The Holy Spirit then begins to work in your life as the painful memory (pus) is released.

2. **The truth about God.**

God is good. He is love. He knows you, better than you know yourself. He has an incredibly high standard that we can't meet on our own. He has promised to change your shameful, wounded, broken, miserable, hardened heart into one that is good and loving. Again, an example of Him turning your weakness into a strength.

> **Ezekiel 36:26** Moreover, I will give you a new heart and put a new spirit within you; and I will remove the heart of stone from your flesh and give you a heart of flesh.

He gave us the person of Jesus to make that happen. He loves YOU. He wants YOU. He needs YOU! Read the Bible: it's like antibiotics attacking the bacteria of your shame.

3. The truth about what God says to YOU.

Your brain can hear the truth, but healing really comes when truth makes its way from your head to your heart. This is where God's miraculous healing happens. You've read His Word, but then His Spirit takes those truths and speaks them to your soul. **His voice penetrates through the hurt and begins the process of making your heart whole again.** You experience that by remaining in His presence and choosing to give Him a chance. Jesus will come into your heart and walk through these situations with you. He will give the peace and courage to walk through these hurts for resolution.

> **Ezekiel 36:25-27** Then I will sprinkle clean water on you, and you will be clean; I will cleanse you from all your filthiness and from all your idols. Moreover, I will give you a new heart and put a new spirit within you; and I will remove the heart of stone from your flesh and give you a heart of flesh. I will put My Spirit within you and cause you to walk in My statutes, and you will be careful to observe My ordinances.

> **Ezekiel 36:33,34** Thus says the Lord God, "On the day that I cleanse you from all your iniquities, I will cause the cities to be inhabited, and the waste places will be rebuilt. The desolate land will be cultivated instead of being a desolation in the sight of everyone who passes by."

Of course, we want it to happen immediately and sometimes it does. I have seen people slain in the Spirit and in His presence for long periods of time. When they "wake up" some will tell stories of Jesus coming and walking with them, taking them through the hurts or shameful situations, and showing them that He was there even though they did not recognize it.

Only God knows the appropriate way of healing for an individual. So often we want it to happen immediately, but at times it comes as a process. The antibiotics of His Word may need time to work. Also, various habit patterns that may have developed from hurts may need correcting. Such habit patterns as anger outbursts, bitterness, negativity, judgmentalism, and avoidance may need to be dealt with. I asked the Lord about this gradual form, and the Holy Spirit directed me to Deuteronomy:

> **Deuteronomy 7:22** The Lord your God will clear away these nations before you little by little; you will not be able to put an end to them quickly, for the wild beasts would grow too numerous for you.

After the Holy Spirit has lanced the abscess and healed the hurt, the enemy will challenge you with similar situations that you were healed from to try to have you respond as you did before. The Holy Spirit will show you how to respond in those situations as you call upon Him, fulfilling the scripture:

> **2 Timothy 2:13** If we are faithless, He remains faithful, for He cannot deny Himself.

What a God we serve, He not only lances the abscess and applies the light of His Word, but He also transforms us into a new creature in Him. In this area of my life that used to be shameful, now I know

God in a very special deep way. The Holy Spirit will bring various people into your life that have experienced similar hurts, and as you share your story, along with the biblical truth shown from His Word, the Holy Spirit will be released, and you will see others touched by God. He takes our weaknesses and turns it into bread whereby we can feed others. The very thing you thought would keep you crippled becomes the banner by which you demonstrate the goodness of God. He turns your weakness into strength as you share what God has done.

So often we want this to happen immediately, but as I noted above, often it takes time. As I questioned the Lord about this gradual form of healing, the HS directed me to Deuteronomy.

Bring your shame into the light. Repent, forgive if He tells you to, and grow in Him. That's where healing is found.

James 5:13-16 (AMP) Confess to another therefore your faults—your slips, your false steps, your offenses, your sins; and pray (also) for one another, that you may be healed and restored—to a spiritual tone of mind and heart. The earnest (heartfelt, continued) prayer of a righteous man makes tremendous power available—dynamic in its working.

Hebrews 4:12-13 for the Word of God is living and active and sharper than any two-edged sword and piercing as far as the division of soul and spirit, of both joints and marrow, and able to judge the thoughts and intentions of the heart. And there is no creature hidden, from His sight, but all things are open and laid bare to the eyes of Him with whom we must do.

1 Thessalonians 5:23 Now may the peace of God Himself sanctify you entirely and may your spirit and soul and body be preserved complete, without blame at the coming of our Lord Jesus Christ.

1 Thessalonians 5:19 Do not quench the Spirit.

Matthew 11:28 Come to Me, all who are weary and heavy-laden, and I will give you rest.

1 John 1:7 but if we walk in the Light as He Himself is in the Light, we have fellowship with one another, and the blood of Jesus His Son cleanses us from all sin.

Philippians 3:14,15 I press on toward the goal for the prize of the upward call of God in Christ Jesus. Let us therefore, as many as are perfect, have this attitude; and if in anything you have a different attitude, God will reveal that also to you.

What a promise of God in Philippians 3. If we keep pressing into Him and growing in Him, at the appropriate time, God will reveal anything that needs to be dealt with. That's the way it was in my own life. I had to grow in God through His Word in order for Him to reveal misunderstandings that I had developed from life's hurts. He is such a loving God that He sent His Holy Spirit to walk with us in order to help us grow in Him.

As you review Psalm 146 and Isaiah 61 (the initiation of Jesus' ministry) again, I believe the Holy Spirit will give you new insight into this ministry of Jesus Christ that is also available for you and me. Often during ministry times I have witnessed that a word of knowledge from the Holy Spirit will be like that scalpel that opens the abscess of shame/hurt and lets the light of Jesus Christ (His Word) into people's lives. All we must do as ministers of His glory is move in the boldness of the Holy Spirit and speak what He reveals and be obedient to Him. That is moving in the ministry of Jesus Christ.

NO MATTER WHAT PAIN (SHAME) YOU HAVE ENDURED—
JESUS KNOWS AND UNDERSTANDS. HE HAS BEEN THROUGH IT
ALL. BECAUSE CHRIST TURNED HIS HURTS TO ADVANTAGE, SO
CAN YOU. YOUR WEAKNESS NOW BECOMES YOUR STRENGTH
IN HIM! JESUS CAME TO HEAL THE BROKENHEARTED AND
DELIVER US FROM SHAME!

Appendix C
CURSES, ABOMINATIONS, AND PERVERSIONS[18,19,20,50-52]

While ministering, the Holy Spirit began giving Donna and me
words about curses. I shared with you the dramatic healings we
witnessed as we spoke out the words of knowledge. The Holy Spirit
began to open a whole new area of understanding to us. It was very
accepted in Asian cultures, but I really struggled with my Western
mind. As I asked God what He was doing and speaking, He began
revealing many scriptures and other resources to us. The revelation
of this section began in the 80s. The more truth we spoke out from
His Word, the more power was released to set people free. As we
share this next section, it is easy to fall into legalism, but I ask you
the reader to pray and ask the Holy Spirit to give you insight and
understanding in this area.

In my time with the Lord, He took me initially to a commonly
quoted scripture.

> **Hosea 4:6** My people are destroyed for lack of knowledge. Because
> you have rejected knowledge, I also will reject you from being My
> priest. Since you have forgotten the law of your God, I also will forget
> your children.

What a powerful scripture. Notice the first part states that people are destroyed because of a lack of knowledge. If a policeman stops me for speeding and I claim ignorance of the speed limit, it usually does me no good. Note the next sentence. Because of rejecting knowledge, one will be rejected from being a priest, a minister of God. That got my attention. It is even more profound because my not knowing or forgetting the law of God will have an influence on my children. That also got my attention. Let's try to get some understanding by looking at other scriptures.

> **Exodus 15:26** And He said, "If you will give earnest heed to the voice of the Lord your God, and do what is right in His sight, and give ear to His commandments, and keep all His statutes, I will put none of the diseases on you which I have put on the Egyptians; for I, the Lord, am your healer."

Recall all the plagues and diseases that the Lord let loose on the Egyptians. As noted in the diagram I am suggesting that certain curses can block the healing power of God. Let us spend some time looking at some scriptures that I will ask you to read in your Bible instead of me reproducing them here.

Let's begin with Deuteronomy. I must admit that I had spent very little time in Deuteronomy, but I found out through reading many sources that Jesus quoted Deuteronomy more than any other scripture. Look at **Deuteronomy 29:14-21.**

> **Verses 14 and 15** relates to a covenant and oath that was made between the children of Israel and God plus those who were not there that day (that is you and me).

> **Verses 16 and 17** talks about walking through the various lands where idols were worshiped.

Verse 18 states that there shall not be found among you anyone who worships these idols and compares them to a poisonous root or wormwood.

Verse 19 deals with the stubborn heart which will turn the lush ground into desert.

Verses 20 and 21 states that the Lord will not forgive him and he will be cursed.

Next, the Holy Spirit took me to what causes curses, and I will share how the Lord began speaking to me in this area of ministry that applied not only to others but also to me. Some of the curses that scripture mentions are:

Deuteronomy 27:15-26

Verse 15 says cursed is the man who makes an idol.

Yes, I understood that but that didn't apply to me. Then the Lord spoke to me and reminded me that my profession had become an idol in my life and that even ministry can replace God. Yes, the Old Testament does speak into today's situations.

Verse 16 says cursed is the man who does not honor his father and mother.

For instance, if I don't forgive my father and mother when they have hurt me, intentionally or unintentionally, then I can be placing a curse on my life.

Verse 17 says cursed is the man who moves his neighbor's boundary mark.

In other words, do not claim your neighbor's land.

Verses 18-26 they essentially go through the Ten Commandments.

They deal with sexual sins, having intercourse within the family, intercourse with animals, striking a neighbor in secret, and accepting bribes. Read them and notice after each the children of Israel all proclaim "Amen." In other words they were proclaiming that they were accepting the statement.

Next the Holy Spirit had me look at the consequences of disobedience, the actual manifestation (symptom) of a curse.

Deuteronomy 28:15 But it shall come about, if you do not obey the Lord your God, to observe to do all His commandments and His statutes with which I charge you today, that all these curses will come upon you and overtake you:

Verse 21,22 The Lord will make the pestilence cling to you until He has consumed you from the land where you are entering to possess it. The Lord will smite you with consumption and with fever and with inflammation and with fiery heat and with the sword and with blight and with mildew, and they will pursue you until you perish.

The thought came to my mind, could some of the illnesses that I had seen as a physician be because of curses? Then I came to:

Verse 27 The Lord will smite you with the boils of Egypt and with tumors and with the scab and with the itch, from which you cannot be healed.

I recalled the women in Malaysia that we discussed in our story who had a dermatological condition that could not be healed until we broke the curse. It was in the Bible all along, but I was ignorant of His Word (Chapter 8).

Verses 28-44

These scriptures deal with all the difficulties that can occur regarding health, property, family, and how you can never have victory but always fail. I then recall friends or relatives who could never succeed and always failed.

> **Verses 38,39** You shall bring out much seed to the field, but you will gather in little, for the locust will consume it. You shall plant and cultivate vineyards, but you will neither drink of the wine nor gather the grapes, for the worm will devour them.

We all know people who always seem to fail. Could this be because of a curse? And finally,

> **Verse 45, 46** So all these curses shall come on you and pursue you and overtake you until you are destroyed, because you would not obey the Lord your God by keeping His commandments and His statutes which He commanded you. They shall become a sign and a wonder on you and your descendants forever.

These two verses are just a restatement of Hosea 4:6. Let us look at more scripture to get a better understanding of what the Lord is speaking to us today. What do we see rampant today on television and even in our children's programing? The occult. What does Scripture say about being involved in the occult?

OCCULT

> **Deuteronomy 18:10-12** There shall not be found among you anyone who makes his son or his daughter pass through the fire, one who

uses divination, one who practices witchcraft, or one who interprets omens, or a sorcerer, or one who casts a spell, or a medium, or a spiritist, or one who calls up the dead. For whoever does these things is detestable to the Lord; and because of these detestable things the Lord your God will drive them out before you.

Anyone involved in witchcraft or the occult must repent, asking for forgiveness and rebuking any effect upon their lives. This is also a very strong generational bondage that must be dealt with. Man is always looking for a spiritual experience because the spiritual void that came as a result of original sin and man's separation from God longs to be filled. God wants that void filled with His Spirit, but man in his search for a spiritual experience is often snared by the occult—Satan's counterfeit. This is a strong bondage and must be dealt with.

Have you been involved in any form of the occult? If so, it needs to be addressed because you could be in bondage. Notice, Scripture talks about being defiled through participation.

Leviticus 19:26 You shall not eat anything with the blood, nor practice divination or soothsaying.

Verse 31 Do not turn to mediums or spiritists; do not seek them out to be defiled by them. I am the Lord your God.

Leviticus 20:6 As for the person who turns to mediums and to spiritists, to play the harlot after them, I will also set My face against that person and will cut him off from among his people.

One must also be careful when traveling and picking up trinkets to bring back home. Many times I have been invited into people's homes and have seen graven images of foreign gods or objects that have been used in pagan worship that they collected when visiting foreign lands. Items sold to tourists are often prayed over by the maker to bring a curse. We have seen strange illnesses as a result of bringing such objects into the home. Once the objects were destroyed along with asking forgiveness and breaking the curse through prayer, the illnesses disappeared. No wonder Scripture talks about being snared for such things are under the ban. We should surround ourselves with things of God and not covet items dedicated to false gods.

> **Deuteronomy 7:25,26** The graven images of their gods you are to burn with fire; you shall not covet the silver or the gold that is on them, nor take it for yourselves, or you will be snared by it, for it is an abomination to the Lord your God. You shall not bring an abomination into your house, and like it come under the ban; you shall utterly detest it and you shall utterly abhor it, for it is something banned.

In response to the ministry of Paul in Ephesus, those involved in witchcraft burned their items fulfilling the above scriptures.

> **Acts 19:19** And many of those who practiced magic brought their books together and began burning them in the sight of everyone; and they counted up the price of them and found it fifty thousand pieces of silver.

As I shared earlier in my story, the Lord has convicted me of items we had in our house that we had to destroy. Are there items in your house that are not pleasing to the Lord and are a snare for you? Ask the Holy Spirit for revelation and He will guide you.

IMPROPER SEXUAL RELATIONSHIPS

Earlier in this discussion we noted many of God's statues had to do with improper sexual relationships. What does scripture have to say about sexual relationships and the things that we see happening in our society today?

> **Hebrews 13:4** Let marriage be held in honor among all, and let the marriage bed be undefiled; for fornicators and adulterers God will judge.

> **Lev 18:6** do not approach a blood relative to uncover nakedness.

> **Verses 7** None of you shall approach any blood relative of his to uncover nakedness; I am the Lord.

> **Verses 8-17** very specific statutes.

Instructions specifically mentioning father, mother, father's wife, your sister, daughter or your father or mother, son's daughter or daughter's daughter, father or mother's sister, father's brother or brother's wife, daughter-in-law, brother's daughter, etc. How often do we see this violated today in our society?

> **Leviticus 20:20,21** if lie with uncle's wife or brother's wife, will be childless.

This last scripture spoke to me since a majority of my medical practice dealt with infertility. Could some of what I saw really be a curse of God? On multiple occasions I received feedback or witnessed a couple become pregnant in answer to prayer once the curse was broken.

Leviticus 18:23 Also you shall not have intercourse with any animal to be defiled with it, nor shall any woman stand before an animal to mate with it; it is a perversion.

I shared with you earlier how God introduced me to this perversion in ministry at a YWAM school (Chapter 7). Bestiality is more prevalent than one might think.

HOMOSEXUALITY

Leviticus 18:22 You shall not lie with a male as one lies with a female; it is an abomination.

Leviticus 20:13 If there is a man who lies with a male as those lie with a woman, both of them have committed a detestable act; they shall be put to death.

What these scriptures say is not a popular message today. Christian morals are being challenged in every way. Even the definition of marriage has been eschewed as it has become acceptable to mean other than just between a man and woman. Marriage, according to the world, now encompasses a man to man and woman to woman.

Deuteronomy 22:5 A woman shall not wear man's clothing, nor a man woman's clothing.

It is easy to become legalistic on this one and say that a woman should not wear pants and I should not wear my English night shirt. God looks at the heart. If you wear the item because you would rather identify and be of the opposite sex rather than the way God created you, that is wrong in the sight of God.

Deuteronomy 23:1 No one who is emasculated, or has his male organ cut off shall enter the assembly of the Lord.

Transgender occurrences are becoming acceptable in the eyes of the world, which is contrary to how we were created by God.

These two following scriptures give us guidance in what we should be doing.

Leviticus 20:7 You shall consecrate yourselves therefore and be holy, for I am the Lord your God. You shall keep My statutes and practice them; I am the Lord who sanctifies you.

Colossians 2:8 See to it that no one takes you captive through philosophy and empty deception, according to the tradition of men, according to the elementary principles of the world, rather than according to Christ.

In 1 Samuel 15 at the end of the chapter, verses 17-23, we see where the prophet Samuel challenges King Saul as to why he did not follow the instructions of the Lord,

1 Samuel 15:18,19 and the Lord sent you on a mission, and said, "Go and utterly destroy the sinners, the Amalekites, and fight against them until they are exterminated." Why then did you not obey the voice of the Lord, but rushed upon the spoil and did what was evil in the sight of the Lord?

Saul responds that he just kept some of the best things to sacrifice to the Lord.

1 Samuel 15:20,21 Then Saul said to Samuel, "I did obey the voice of the Lord, and went on the mission on which the Lord sent me, and have brought back Agag the king of Amalek, and have utterly destroyed the

Amalekites. But the people took some of the spoil, sheep and oxen, the choicest of the things devoted to destruction, to sacrifice to the Lord your God at Gilgal."

Samuel then makes a profound statement which has implications for us today.

1 Samuel 15:22.23 Samuel said, "Has the Lord as much delight in burnt offerings and sacrifices as in obeying the voice of the Lord? Behold, to obey is better than sacrifice, and to heed than the fat of rams. For rebellion is as the sin of divination, and insubordination is as iniquity and idolatry. Because you have rejected the word of the Lord, He has also rejected you from being king."

We must be careful if we are servants of God to follow His words and directions completely and not move in rebellion and insubordination. This is so easy to do.

GENERATIONAL SINS

As we have noted earlier, the Holy Spirit began to give us words of knowledge regarding sins of the forefathers. As we would pray and break these bondages, we witnessed people being set free. There again, that did not make sense to us, so we went back to Scripture to get understanding.

Jeremiah 31:29 The fathers have eaten sour grapes, and the children's teeth are set on edge.

Exodus 20:3-5 You shall have no other gods before Me. You shall not make for yourself an idol...visiting the iniquity of the fathers on the children, on the third and the fourth generations of those who hate Me....

Deuteronomy 23:3-5 No Ammonite or Moabite shall enter the assembly of the Lord; none of their descendants, even to the tenth generation, shall ever enter the assembly of the Lord.

Deuteronomy 28:45,46 So all these curses shall come on you and pursue you and overtake you until you are destroyed...They shall become a sign and a wonder on you and your descendants forever.

1 Samuel 15:17-23 The story of Saul not obeying the word of the Lord regarding the Amalekites which we mentioned above and the subsequent effect of rebellion upon the house of Saul.

Genesis 3 and 4 The story of Adam and Eve and original sin which resulted in introducing sickness, death, and murder into their family (Cain murdering his brother Abel). We still deal with Adam's sin and the resulting curses.

Genesis 9 Noah's drunkenness: led to his son Ham dishonoring him. As the result of this curse, an entire lineage of people were and still are under a curse in the land of Canaan.

Genesis 16 Abraham: went against God's will for him and fathered a son in the flesh; this robbed the birthright from the firstborn son, which went on for the next three generations, and in the next five generations the youngest prospered instead of the oldest.

Genesis 20 We also see Abraham lying to Abimelech and a spirit of lying and deception manifesting in his children. Jacob lied to his father concerning his birthright. His sons in turn lied to him about the disappearance of Joseph.

2 Samuel 11 David: the man after God's own heart, fell into sexual sin with Bathsheba. He committed adultery and then had her husband Uriah murdered to cover up his sexual sin. As a result, we see a history of incest, rape, rebellion, and womanizing in his children.

2 Samuel 12:13-14 When looking at the sin of David and Bathsheba, we also must look at the term CONSEQUENCE OF SIN. The first-born child died because of the consequence of their sin. In other words, we may well suffer from the consequence of our sins or our forefathers'.

Leonard Ravenhill in his book *America Is Too Young*[53] contrasts two different family inheritances by comparing the descendants of an atheist versus those of a Christian.

Max Jukes, [an] atheist:

He lived a godless life. He married an ungodly woman, and from this union there were 310 who died as paupers, 150 were criminals, 7 were murderers, 100 were drunkards, and more than half of the women were prostitutes. His 540 descendants cost the state 1.25 million dollars.

A great man of God, Jonathan Edwards (1703-1758):

He lived at the same time as Max Jukes, but he married a godly woman. Of his 1,394 descendants, 13 became college presidents, 65 college professors, 3 United States Senators, 30 judges, 100 lawyers, 60 physicians, 75 army and navy officers, 100 preachers and missionaries, 60 authors of prominence, one VP of the US, 80 public officials, 295 college graduates, among whom were governors of states and ministers to foreign countries. His descendants did not cost the state a penny. This is quite a contrast of the two families.

I previously mentioned the effect of Freemasonry on my life. Although I had never participated, it was in my family line. I asked for forgiveness for my father's and family's involvement in this secret society and for my mother's involvement in the Eastern Star, breaking any effect upon my life or that of my children. For further reading on this subject, I would recommend John Ankerberg and John Weldon's book.[54]

When we consider generational sins, remember we are a tri-part being—body, soul, and spirit. In the physical realm we receive genes from our parents that determine such things as skin, hair, eye color, and other physical features (some may be bad features, as in deformities). Physical genes may also skip generations and show up unexpectedly. You may hear someone say something like, "Our baby has fiery red hair, and we have no idea where that came from." If you looked back in the genealogy, you would be sure to find that missing link.

In the soulish realm we are influenced by family traits and pick up attitudes, mannerisms, prejudices, likes and dislikes (some of these may be bad as well).

In the spirit realm, things are also handed down from generation to generation in what I call "spiritual genes" (some good as well as some bad). Some of the bad things we can receive generationally are rejection, alcoholism, divorcee, anger, suicide, and the effect of generational involvement in the occult. Just as in the physical realm, these "spiritual genes" can also skip generations.

When the HS first had us start praying to break off the sins of the forefathers, this seemed to be contrary to everything that I had been taught. Once we came to Jesus, was this not all covered by the blood of the Lamb? But as people confessed the sins of the forefathers, they were set free. To get some understanding of this area, I again went back to the Word. Let us look at two righteous kings who brought the children of Israel back into relationship with God.

In **2 Chronicles 29** King Hezekiah and in 2 Chronicles 34 King Josiah both brought the children of Israel back into relationship with God. They both had the children of Israel repent, consecrate themselves (outwardly tore their clothes as a sign), consecrate the temple, and apply the blood sacrifice. That certainty makes sense for sins that they themselves did, but what about their forefathers? Scripture gives us insights.

Leviticus 26:40 If they confess their iniquity and the iniquity of their forefathers....

:42 then I will remember My covenant.

:44 I will not reject them.

Ezekiel 18:14 Now behold, he has a son who has observed all his father's sins which he committed and observing does not do likewise.

:17 ...he executes My ordinances and walks in My statutes; he will not die for his father's iniquity, he will surely live.

:32 ...Therefore repent and live

Thus, these two righteous kings had the children of Israel repent for not only their own actual sins but also for the sins of their forefathers. They then did the blood sacrifice. That is what we must do today except our blood sacrifice is the Lord Jesus Christ.

Galatians 3:13 Christ redeemed us from the curse of the Law, having become a curse for us—for it is written, "CURSED IS EVERYONE WHO HANGS ON A TREE"—

Matthew 5:17 Do not think that I came to abolish the Law or the Prophets; I did not come to abolish, but to fulfill.

In **Hebrews 9 and 10** we see the importance of the blood sacrifice. In the Old Testament that of animals was used whereas in the New Testament it is the blood of Jesus Christ.

HOW TO BREAK A CURSE [17,18-20,50-52,55,56]

In summary then, how do we deal with our actual sins and the sins of our forefathers that have resulted in a curse?

REPENT AND FORSAKE

Joel 2:12-13 Yet even now, declares the Lord, return to Me with all your heart, and with fasting, weeping, and mourning; and render your heart and not your garments. Now return to the Lord your God, for He is gracious and compassionate, slow to anger, abounding in loving-kindness, and relenting of evil.

Proverbs 28:13 He who conceals his transgressions will not prosper, but he who confesses and forsakes then will find compassion.

If the Holy Spirit reveals a consequence of sin (curse) resulting from your own sin or that of your forefathers, you must ask for forgiveness (repent) and rebuke (forsake) the consequence of the sin on you or that of your family.

BLESSINGS

Deuteronomy 28:1-14

Now it shall be, if you diligently obey the LORD your God, being careful to do all His commandments which I command you today, the LORD your God will set you high above all the nations of the earth. All these blessings will come upon you and overtake you if you obey the LORD your God:

Blessed shall you be in the city, and blessed shall you be in the country.

Blessed shall be the offspring of your body and the produce of your ground and the offspring of your beasts, the increase of your herd and the young of your flock.

Blessed shall be your basket and your kneading bowl.

Blessed shall you be when you come in and blessed shall you be when you go out.

The LORD shall cause your enemies who rise up against you to be defeated before you; they will come out against you one way and will flee before you seven ways. The LORD will command the blessing upon you in your barns and in all that you put your hand to, and He will bless you in the land which the LORD your God gives you. The LORD will establish you as a holy people to Himself, as He swore to you, if you keep the commandments of the LORD your God and walk in His ways. So all the peoples of the earth will see that you are called by the name of the LORD, and they will be afraid of you. The LORD will make you abound in prosperity, in the offspring of your body and in the offspring of your beast and in the produce of your ground, in the land which the LORD swore to your fathers to give you. The LORD will open for you His good storehouse, the heavens, to give rain to your land in its season and to bless all the work of your hand; and you shall lend to many nations, but you shall not borrow. The LORD will make you the head and not the tail, and you only will be above, and you will not be underneath, if you listen to the commandments of the LORD your God, which I charge you today, to observe them carefully, and do not turn aside from any of the words which I command you today, to the right or to the left, to go after other gods to serve them.

Deuteronomy 30:2 return to the Lord.

:5 …He will prosper you more than your father.

:6 ...will circumcise your heart and the heart of your children.

:15 See I have set before you today life and prosperity, and death and adversity.

:19...I have set before you life and death, the blessing and the curse. So choose life in order that you may live, you and your descendants (emphasis is mine).

Understanding of the statutes and ordinances of God, along with His blessings, offers a better understanding of the following scriptures.

Psalm 47:4 He chooses our inheritance for us, the glory of Jacob whom He loves. Selah.

1 Peter 1:3,4 Blessed be the God and Father of our Lord Jesus Christ, who according to His great mercy has caused us to be born again to a living hope through the resurrection of Jesus Christ from the dead, to obtain an inheritance which is imperishable and undefiled and will not fade away, reserved in heaven for you,

Hebrews 2:14,15 Therefore, since the children share in flesh and blood, He Himself likewise also partook of the same, that through death He might render powerless him who had the power of death, that is, the devil, and might free those who through fear of death were subject to slavery all their lives.

Has the Holy Spirit revealed something to you today from which you want to be set free? This is especially true if you or any of your family has had any involvement in the occult. Now is the time to be set free. Thank God for His revelation of the actual sin/ or generational sins in your life. Then repent, ask for forgiveness

for what you or your family's involvement has been, and rebuke the consequence of the sin.

Appendix D
DELIVERANCE[11,16,18,20,45,50-52,55,56]

> **Mark 16:15-20 (MSG)** Then He said to them, "Go into the world. Go everywhere and announce the Message of God's good news to one and all. Whoever believes and is baptized is saved; whoever refuses to believe is damned. These are some of the signs that will accompany believers: They will throw out demons in My name, they will speak in new tongues, they will take snakes in their hands, they will drink poison and not be hurt, they will lay hands on the sick and make them well." Then the Master Jesus, after briefing them, was taken up to heaven, and He sat down beside God in the place of honor. And the disciples went everywhere preaching, the Master working right with them, validating the Message with indisputable evidence.

This Message version leaves no doubt that followers of Jesus are to be involved in deliverance. This is an area that I did not want to be involved in, yet to avoid it meant that I was disregarding 30 percent of the ministry of Jesus. Donna and I do not look for a demonic presence but will deal with it if present. Many times as the Lord brings healing to an emotional hurt, the Holy Spirit will reveal that the wound has been "infected" by a demotic spirit. When that is brought to light, it is cast out by using the authority of Jesus Christ. So often a wounded person's symptoms are superficially dealt with and the "infection" is not cleaned out and the "infection" remains. There is no true healing.

> **Jeremiah 6:14** They have healed the brokenness of My people superficially, saying, "Peace, peace," But there is no peace.

Wounds are covered but not cleansed. You must probe the wound in the anointing of the Holy Spirit for evil spirits to be detected. As we shared with our friend Ellen, as we prayed the enemy revealed himself and the name of Jesus set our friend free and healed her. Again and again in public meetings as the Word goes forth and the anointing of God is present, the enemy will manifest itself and you must exercise the authority of Jesus Christ.

Joel 2:32 Whosoever shall call upon the name of the Lord shall be delivered.

Joel 1:4; 2:25 The invading arm of locusts will be driven out. God's people will be delivered.

HOW JESUS DEALT WITH DEMONS

With Jesus as our example, let us look at a few scriptures to get insight as to how He dealt with demons.

Mark 1:39 So He continued preaching in their synagogues and expelling evil spirits through the whole of Galilee.

Mark 1:27-28 They were all amazed, so that they debated among themselves, saying, "What is this? A new teaching with authority! He commands even the unclean spirits, and they obey Him." Immediately the news about Him spread everywhere into all the surrounding district of Galilee.

1. The way Jesus dealt with demons was a striking feature of His ministry.

2. The people of Jesus' day recognized the reality of demons and practiced some form of exorcism. Jesus' authority was new and

even the demons recognized Jesus and those going in His name and anointing.

a. **Matthew 12:27-29** If I by Beelzebub cast out demons, by whom do your sons cast them out? For this reason, they will be your judges. But if I cast out demons by the Spirit of God, then the kingdom of God has come upon you. Or how can anyone enter the strong man's house and carry off his property, unless he first binds the strong man? And then he will plunder his house.

b. **Acts 19:13-15** But also some of the Jewish exorcists, who went from place to place, attempted to name over those who had the evil spirits the name of the Lord Jesus, saying, "I adjure you by Jesus whom Paul preaches." Seven sons of one Sceva, a Jewish chief priest, were doing this. And the evil spirit answered and said to them, "I recognize Jesus, and I know about Paul, but who are you?"

c. **Mark 1:24-25** "What business do we have with each other, Jesus of Nazareth? Have you come to destroy us? I know who You are—the Holy One of God!" And Jesus rebuked him, saying, "Be quiet, and come out of him!"

3. Jesus Himself described the clash between two spiritual kingdoms. **Matthew 12:28** But if I cast out demons by the Spirit of God, then the kingdom of God has come upon you.

4. At times Jesus spoke directly to demons, and they to Him. But there was no New Testament pattern for holding lengthy conversations with them.

a. **Mark 3:11-12** Whenever the unclean spirits saw Him, they would fall down before Him and shout, "You are the Son of God!" And He earnestly warned them not to tell who He was.

b. **Mark 5:6-13** Seeing Jesus from a distance, he ran up and bowed down before Him; and shouting with a loud voice, he *said, "What business do we have with each other, Jesus, Son of the Most High God? I implore You by God, do not torment me!" For He had been saying to him, "Come out of the man, you unclean spirit!" And He was asking him, "What is your name?" And he *said to Him, "My name is Legion; for we are many." And he began to implore Him earnestly not to send them out of the country. Now there was a large herd of swine feeding nearby on the mountain. The demons implored Him, saying, "Send us into the swine so that we may enter them." Jesus gave them permission. And coming out, the unclean spirits entered the swine; and the herd rushed down the steep bank into the sea, about two thousand of them; and they were drowned in the sea.

5. There were powerful physical manifestations when Jesus cast out demons.

a. **Mark 1:26** Throwing him into convulsions, the unclean spirit cried out with a loud voice and came out of him.

b. **Mark 3:11** Whenever the unclean spirits saw Him, they would fall down before Him and shout, "You are the Son of God!"

c. **Mark 9:20,26-27** They brought the boy to Him. When he saw Him, immediately the spirit threw him into a convulsion, and falling to the ground, he began rolling around and foaming at the mouth.... After crying out and throwing him into terrible convulsions, it came out; and the boy became so much like a corpse that most of them said, "He is dead!" But Jesus took him by the hand and raised him; and he got up.

    d. Similar manifestation in the ministry of Philip in Samaria. **Acts 8:7** For in the case of many who had unclean spirits, they were coming out of them shouting with a loud voice; and many who had been paralyzed and lame were healed.

6. Jesus never commanded demons to go to hell or the pit.

    a. **Mark 1:25-26** And Jesus rebuked him, saying, "Be quiet, and come out of him!" Throwing him into convulsions, the unclean spirit cried out with a loud voice and came out of him.

    b. Jesus left demons free to enter any other bodies that were available to them. **Luke 8:31-33** They were imploring Him not to command them to go away into the abyss. Now there was a herd of many swine feeding there on the mountain; and the demons implored Him to permit them to enter the swine. And He gave them permission. And the demons came out of the man and entered the swine; and the herd rushed down the steep bank into the lake and was drowned.

    c. There is a time ordained when evil spirits will be bound and punished.

Revelation 20:2,3,10 And he laid hold of the dragon, the serpent of old, who is the devil and Satan, and bound him for a thousand years; and he threw him into the abyss, and shut it and sealed it over him, so that he would not deceive the nations any longer, until the thousand years were completed; after these things he must be released for a short time.... And the devil who deceived them was thrown into the lake of fire and brimstone, where the beast and the false prophet are also; and they will be tormented day and night forever and ever.

7. Both Jesus and the demons recognized that this time has not yet come. **Matthew 8:29** And they cried out, saying, "What business do we have with each other, Son of God? Have You come here to torment us before the time?"

8. At times Jesus laid hands on or spoke a word to people who had demons.

   a. **Luke 4:40-41** While the sun was setting, all those who had any who were sick with various diseases brought them to Him; and laying His hands on each one of them, He was healing them. Demons also were coming out of many, shouting, "You are the Son of God!" But rebuking them, He would not allow them to speak, because they knew Him to be the Christ.

   b. **Luke 13:11-13** Jesus laid hands on the woman with a spirit of infirmity.

   c. **Matthew 8:16** When evening came, they brought to Him many who were demon-possessed; and He cast out the spirits with a word and healed all who were ill.

9. Normally those who needed deliverance had to submit themselves to the ministry of Jesus.

   a. **Mark 1:21-24** They *went into Capernaum; and immediately on the Sabbath He entered the synagogue and began to teach. They were amazed at His teaching; for He was teaching them as one having authority, and not as the scribes. Just then there was a man in their synagogue with an unclean spirit; and he cried out, saying, "What business do we have with each other, Jesus of Nazareth? Have You come to destroy us? I know who You are—the Holy One of God!"

b. **Mark 5:6,7** Seeing Jesus from a distance, he ran up and bowed down before Him; and shouting with a loud voice, he *said, "What business do we have with each other, Jesus, Son of the Most High God? I implore You by God, do not torment me!"

10. In the case of a child with a demon, Jesus required faith on the part of a parent.

a. **Mark 9:22-23** "It has often thrown him both into the fire and into the water to destroy him. But if You can do anything, take pity on us, and help us!" And Jesus said to him, "'If You can?' All things are possible to him who believes."

b. Also see the gentile women in **Mark 7:25-30.**

11. Jesus encouraged those who were delivered from demons to testify of their deliverance, and they were not ashamed to do so. **Mark 5:18-21** As He was getting into the boat, the man who had been demon-possessed was imploring Him that he might accompany Him. And He did not let him, but He *said to him, "Go home to your people and report to them what great things the Lord has done for you, and how He had mercy on you." And he went away and began to proclaim in Decapolis what great things Jesus had done for him; and everyone was amazed.

12. Finally, Jesus never sent anyone out to preach the gospel without giving them the authority to cast out demons. **Mark 3:15** and to

have authority to cast out the demons. Also see **Matthew 10:1-8; Luke 10:17; Mark 3: 6:12-13; 16:15-18.**

There is much confusion concerning the possibility of a Christian having a demon. Let's look at terminology. The Greek word for devil is *diablos,* meaning slanderer. The Greek word for demon is *diamon* or *diamonion*: to HAVE an unclean/evil spirit, or to be UNDER THE INFLUENCE OF. The better term is: DEMONIZED. In certain Bible translations, the term demon is used interchangeably with "evil spirit" or "unclean spirit" and is translated as being possessed, which denotes being completely taken over. The word *possessed* is misleading. Derek Prince[16,18] and Francis MacNutt[52] go into depth regarding this.

(Matthew 4:24; 8:16, 28, 33; 9:32; 12:22; 14:22; Mark 1:32; 5:15, 16, 18; Luke 8:36). A certain part of one's personality could be demonized because of open doors through hurts, unforgiveness, sin, etc. Demons can also manifest physically as was seen in Ellen's case. One can be free in certain parts of their life but bound in others. There would not be confusion if the word *possession* had been translated properly as *demonized.*

As one grows in God's Word in understanding His character, grace, and love, the Holy Spirit will reveal areas in your life that need to be dealt with. This fulfills the scripture:

Philippians 3:14,15 I press on toward the goal for the prize of the upward call of God in Christ Jesus. Let us therefore, as many as are perfect, have this attitude; and if in anything you have a different attitude, God will reveal that also to you.

What a promise of God. I continue to press into Him, but if there is an area of my life that is not in Him, He will reveal it at the appropriate time. That is the God we serve. For a more in-depth discussion refer to the Sanfords' book (John Sandford and Mark Sanford, *Deliverance and Inner Healing*, Chosen Books, 2008).[45]

HOW DO BONDAGES BEGIN?

Proverbs 5:22,23 His own iniquities will capture the wicked, and he will be held with the cords of his sin. He will die for lack of instruction, and in the greatness of his folly he will go astray.

Every time there is sin, it is an opportunity for demonic infiltration. This contrasts with

Ecclesiastes 8:5 He who keeps a royal command experiences no trouble, for a wise heart knows the proper time and procedure.

John 8:31-32 Jesus therefore was saying to those Jews who had believed Him, "If you abide in My word, then you are truly disciples of Mine; and you shall know the truth, and the truth shall make you free."

Fortunately, the grace of God protects us many times, but if sin is involved, that sin opens the door for the enemy to come in.

Conditions that prepare the way for demonic infiltration.

1. **LACK OF THE WORD (Matthew 12:43-45)** Now when the unclean spirit goes out of a man, it passes through waterless places, seeking rest, and does not find it. Then it says, "I will return to my house from which I came"; and when it comes, it finds it unoccupied, swept, and put in order. Then it goes and takes along with it seven other spirits more wicked than itself, and they go in and live there; and the last state of that man

becomes worse than the first. That is the way it will also be with this evil generation.

Ezekiel 34: People are destroyed because the shepherds are not feeding the sheep.

2. **UNFORGIVENESS (Mathew 18:34)** And his lord, moved with anger, handed him over to the torturers until he should repay all that was owed him. So shall My heavenly Father also do to you, if each of you does not forgive his brother from your heart.

3. **CARNAL MIND (Romans 8:6)** For the mind set on the flesh is death, but the mind set on the Spirit is life and peace.

4. **PROFANE LANGUAGE WILL DESTROY (2 Timothy 2:16)** But avoid worldly and empty chatter, for it will lead to further ungodliness.

5. **BITTERNESS WILL DESTROY (Hebrews 12:15)** See to it that no one comes short of the grace of God; that no root of bitterness springing up causes trouble, and by it many be defiled.

6. **OCCULT (Deutronomy18:10,11)** There shall not be found among you anyone who makes his son or his daughter pass through the fire, one who uses divination, one who practices witchcraft, or one who interprets omens, or a sorcerer, or one who casts a spell, or a medium, or a spiritist, or one who calls up the dead.

7. **REBELLION (1 Samuel 15:23)** For rebellion is as the sin of divination and insubordination is as iniquity and idolatry. Because you have rejected the word of the Lord, He has also rejected you from being king.

8. **SLANDER (Psalm 101:5)** Whoever secretly slanders his neighbor, him I will destroy; no one who has a haughty look and an arrogant heart will I endure.

9. **LAZINESS (Proverbs15:19)** They way of the sluggard is as a hedge of thorns, but the path of the upright is a highway. **Proverbs 24:30** I passed by the field of the sluggard, and by the vineyard of the man lacking sense.

10. **WRONG CONFESSION (Proverbs 12:13)** An evil man is snared by the transgression of his lips, but the righteous will escape from trouble.

11. **TEMPTATIONS (James 1:1-18)** ...each one is tempted when, by his own evil desire, he is dragged away and enticed.

The fall of Adam and Eve was one of Satan's greatest achievements, and his tactics of deception, accusation, and strategies have not changed for us. The fruit of the tree was good for food (an appeal to the physical being); it was pleasing to the eye (an appeal to the aesthetic being); and desirable for gaining wisdom (an appeal to the intellectual being) **(Genesis 3:6 and Colossians 2:8)**

It is through these three avenues that Satan achieves some of his greatest conquests. Note: He tempts through the things we like, not the things we don't like. For an in-depth discussion, refer to Derek Prince,[16,18] who goes into detail outlining three main forms of Satan's bondage: domination of one person by another (witchcraft, spirits other than Holy Spirit), departures from the Christian faith (heresies by seducing spirits and false teachers), and false religions.

COMMON SNARES OF THE ENEMY

Ouija board

Fortune telling

Mediums

Clairvoyants

Meditation

Oriental cults and philosophies (yoga)

Reincarnation

Astrology

Horoscopes

Hypnosis

Automatic writing

Pharmacia (drugs, alcoholic drinks, sedatives, pep tablets, painkillers)

Psalm 139:21-22 We must decide to hate these enemies of God and their influence in our lives.

Acts 19:17-19 How believers must renounce these forbidden practices and sever all contact.

INSTRUCTIONS WILL LEAD TO DELIVERANCE

Instructions that will lead to deliverance are noted amply by

2 Timothy 2:24-26 And the Lord's bond-servant must not be quarrelsome, but be kind to all, able to teach, patient when wronged, with gentleness correcting those who are in opposition, if perhaps God may grant them repentance leading to the knowledge of the truth, and they may come to their senses and escape from the snare of the devil, having been held captive by him to do his will.

For a more in-depth discussion in this area of deliverance, I would highly recommend any of the following resources[11,16,18-20,45,50-52,55]. From our experience and these resources, a general guide for deliverance is as follows:

PRAYER FOR DELIVERANCE

1. **Be guided by the Holy Spirit.** It is important to have a team that is accustomed to working and praying together. Donna and I have done this together for many years. Do not have people involved that are there for curiosity.

2. Personally, affirm faith in Jesus Christ, especially the one being ministered to, claiming the protection of the blood of Jesus upon everyone there, and intercede for their family and possessions.

3. Humble yourself and ask God if there is anything that He wants to reveal, anything that needs to be confessed, or forgiveness that needs to be spoken. It is important to speak things out loud. One is using that same creative power of God and speaking freedom.

4. Proclamations need to be spoken out as the Holy Spirit reveals them to the individual or those ministering: **confession of sins He reveals, and forgiving those who have hurt or offended (important to break bitterness).** Sometimes people have a hard time with the forgiveness and may have to ask God to help them forgive.

5. If the individual or family has been **involved in the occult** (very important) or any false religions, then they must sever all ties and ask for forgiveness. Also, it is important to destroy any objects associated with the occult or false religions.

6. Ask the Holy Spirit if any curse has been placed upon the individual. If so, thank Jesus for the power of the cross to be released from the curse. Many people pick up souvenirs which have been dedicated to false gods that will put a curse upon anyone owning that object. Also, if the individual cursed someone, the Holy Spirit would often bring this to mind, and it must be spoken out and nullified by the cross.[18-20]

7. Move into a time of rebuking Satan's demons that were revealed.

8. Then speak to any demons that have control over your life and command them to leave (speak out loud and directly to them). "I command you to go now, in the name of Jesus" (expel them).

Submit to the Lord Jesus Christ and resist the devil!

Quite often this is a process which takes time as noted in

Deuteronomy 8:22,23 And the Lord your God will clear away these nations before you little by little; you will not be able to put an end to them quickly; lest the wild beast grow too numerous for you. But the Lord your God shall deliver them before you, and will throw them into great confusion until they are destroyed.

Inner healing and deliverance often occur together. The enemy knows the weaknesses of the individual and will try to use those weaknesses to regain back the territory that he lost. The individual will find that they need to develop new habit patterns. Ask the Lord to show you how to respond differently.

Victory proclamations to resist the enemy:

Obadiah 17: But on Mount Zion there shall be deliverance, and there shall be holiness;

The house of Jacob shall possess their possessions.

2 Corinthians 5:17 Therefore if any man is in Christ, he is a new creature; the old things passed away; behold, new things have come.

1 Thessalonians 5:23 Now may the peace of God Himself sanctify you entirely, and may your spirit and body be preserved complete, without blame at the coming of the Lord Jesus Christ.

1 John 1:9 If we confess our sins, He is faithful and righteous to forgive us our sins and to cleanse us from all unrighteousness.

For more in-depth readings refer to the references cited at the beginning of this appendix.

Appendix E
OVERCOME BY THE SPIRIT (SLAIN IN THE SPIRIT) [57-60]

Over the years, we have seen the Lord use the phenomenon of falling down under the power of God to build faith. When this happens, people become acutely aware that the Spirit of God is present and will seek Him and His presence. What may happen to the individual slain in the Spirit?

1. Externally: body grows weak and falls to the ground. Purpose often is a demonstration of God's power. Sometimes He also uses this manifestation to humble an individual.

2. Internally: it is often a matter of people yielding to the power of God.

3. Internally: may have a spiritual experience. Individuals often relate that Jesus was walking with them through different parts of their lives, healing them, giving them revelations, visions.

4. Internally and externally: sometimes dramatic healings occur.

5. Release from demonic forces.

One does not have to fall down to be blessed by God. You can be in the presence of God without being slain. It is only a sign. Let's get some insight from scriptures about this anointing and biblical evidence.

> **Romans 8:26,27** And in the same way the Spirit also helps our weakness; for we do not know how to pray as we should, but the Spirit Himself intercedes for us with groaning too deep for words; and he who searches the hearts knows what the mind of the Spirit is, because He intercedes for the saints according to the will of God.

> **1 John 2:20** But you have an anointing from the Holy One, and you all know.

> **1 John 2:27** And as for you, the anointing which you received from Him abides in you, and you have no need for anyone to teach you; but as His anointing teaches you about all things, and is true and is not a lie, and just as it has taught you, you abide in Him.

Is there any biblical evidence of this phenomena?

> **Revelation 1:17** the apostle John, who was in the Spirit, received a revelation of Jesus Christ and "fell at His feet as a dead man."

> **2 Chronicles 5:13,14** The house of the Lord was filled with a cloud, so that the priests could not stand to minister because of the cloud, for the glory of the Lord filled the house.

> **Acts 9:3-5** Paul's Road to Damascus experience: ...and he fell to the ground.

Acts 22:17,18 Paul in Jerusalem: "It came about when I returned to Jerusalem and was praying in the temple, that I feel into a trance, and I saw Him saying to me, 'Make haste, and get out of Jerusalem quickly.'"

Acts 10:10 on a rooftop in Joppa the apostle Peter "fell into a trance" in which Lord gave him a vision.

Daniel 8:17,18 The prophet Daniel heard God speaking to him, and he "sank into a deep sleep."

Acts 5:12 Many signs and wonders were taking place.

Mark 16:20 confirmed the word by the signs that follow.

1 Corinthians12:4 now there are varieties of gifts, but the same spirit.

Let's look at some examples in history.

1. Jonathan Edwards (1707-1785) wrote that people at his meetings in the First Great Awakening "fainted" and "swooned."

2. John Wesley (1703-1791) preached, and people fell to the ground. One observer gives this report of a Wesley service in southern England: "He was preaching at Bristol, to people who cried as in the agonies of death, who were struck to the ground and lay there groaning, who were released with a visible struggle then and there from the power of the devil."[57]

3. Multitudes fell during the preaching of the great evangelists George Whitefield (1714-1770) and John Asbury (1745-1816): a Calvinist and a Methodist.

4. Second Great Awakening (1799) A Presbyterian minister came to the Cane Ridge meeting of that revival and observed: "At one time I saw at least 500, swept down in a moment, as if a battery

of a thousand guns had been opened upon them. Truly these people lie there as if slain by the Spirit."[58]

5. Charles Finney (1792-1875) people fell out of their chairs while he preached. Finney wrote about this experience: "The mind sees truth, unveiled, and in such relations is ready to take away all bodily strength, while the mind looks in upon the unveiled glories of the Godhead. The veil seems to be removed from the mind, and the truth is seen much as we must suppose it to be when the Spirit is disembodied. No wonder this should overpower the body."[59]

6. Common in the ministry of Kathryn Kuhlman, Reinhard Bonnke and Benny Hinn.

7. Frances MacNutt,[60] "The great revivals should serve as a reminder: They featured Spirit empowered preaching accompanied by listeners fainting, shouting, and dropping to the ground as if felled by a giant cannon shot. Who can miss the point that wc are simply weak human beings in the presence of a mighty God? When we fall under the power, God is knocking us off our feet in a prophetic action demanding that we relinquish control over our lives—and over the church to Him."

Why would God use somethings like this ridiculous experience like slipping on a banana peel? Paul told Timothy that a time would come when we would maintain the form of religion but deny the great power of it. Thus, falling under the power has a prophetic impact. We become instantly aware that God's power is made manifest in our weakness. We are asked to let go of our controls.

2 Timothy 3:5 holding to a form of godliness, although they have denied its power.

The glory of the Lord is filling the temple, and we are the temple of the Holy Spirit.

> **2 Corinthians 6:16** For we are the temple of the living God; just as God said, "I will dwell in them and walk among them; and shall be their God, and they shall be My people."

> **John 1:14** And the Word became flesh, and dwelt among us, and we beheld His glory, glory as of the only begotten from the Father, full of grace and truth.

As we mentioned in the previous chapter, as one comes into the presence of the glory of God, there may be demonic manifestations. His presence will drive demons to the surface.

> **Luke 9:41,42** And Jesus answered and said, "O unbelieving and perverted generation, how long shall I be with you, and put up with you? Bring your son here." And while he was still approaching, the demon dashed him to the ground, and threw him into a convulsion. But Jesus rebuked the unclean spirit, and healed the boy, and gave him back to his father.

> **Luke 4:31-35** And He came down to Capernaum, a city of Galilee. And He was teaching them on the Sabbath; and they were amazed at His teaching, for His message was with authority. And there was a man in the synagogue possessed by the spirit of an unclean demon, and he cried out with a loud voice, "Ha! What do we have to do with You, Jesus of Nazareth? And Jesus rebuked him, saying, "Be quiet and come out of him!"

What happened in the OT: amazing things will happen when the glory of God is manifest.

2 Chronicles 7:1-3 The Shekinah Gory: Now when Solomon had finished praying, fire came down from heaven and consumed the burnt offering and the sacrifices; and the glory of the Lord filled the house. And the priests could not enter into the house of the Lord, because the glory of the Lord filled the Lord's house. And all the sons of Israel, seeing the fire come down and the gory of the Lord upon the house, bowed down on the pavement with their faces to the ground, and they worshiped and gave praise to the Lord, saying "Truly He is good, truly His lovingkindness is everlasting."

In summary, then, how does God use this experience?

1. Builds Faith

2. Signifies yielding to God, or He humbles man

3. Healing (physical and emotional)

4. Demonic manifestations and deliverance

Bibliography

1. Ralph and Allene Wilkerson. *Greater Works! Why Not Now?*, Beyond Productions Inc., Dana Point, CA, 2001.

2. Oral Roberts, *Daily Blessing: A Guide to Seed-Faith Living,* Revell, 1978.

3. Oral Roberts. *Unleashing the Power of Praying in the Spirit.* Harrison House, Tulsa, OK, 1993.

4. Oral Roberts. *Expect a Miracle: My Life and Ministry: An Autobiography.* Thomas Nelson Inc, Nashville, TN, 1995.

5. Loren Cunningham. *Is That Really You, God?: Hearing the Voice of God.* YWAM Publishing, Seattle, WA, 2001.

6. Bob Yandian Ministries, www.bobyandian.com

7. Jack Hayford. *Manifest Presence: Expecting a Visitation of God's Grace Through Worship.* Chosen Books, Grand Rapids, MI 2005.

8. S. David Moore. *Pastor Jack: The Authorized Biography.* David C. Cook, Colorado Spring, CO, 2020.

9. Jack Winters. *The Home Coming.* YWAM Publishing, Seattle, WA, 1997.

10. Noel and Phyl Gibson. *Excuse Me Your Rejection Is Showing.* Sovereign World, 1993.

11. Noel and Phyl Gibson. *Evicting Demonic Squatters and Breaking Bondages.* Freedom in Christ Ministries Trust, Drummoyne, NSW, Australia, 1987.

12. Dr. Bruce Thompson and Barbara Thompson. *Walls of My Heart.* Crown Ministries International, Euclid, MN, 1989.

13. Dean Sherman. *Spiritual Warfare for Every Christian.* YWAM Publishing, Seattle, WA, 1990.

14. Bob Yandian. *Romans: A New Testament Commentary.* Harrison House Inc, Tulsa, OK, 2015.

15. Ernest F. Crocker, MD. *Nine Minutes Past Midnight.* Authentic Publishers, Franklin, TN, 2013.

16. Derek Prince. *They Shall Expel Demons,* Chosen Books, Grand Rapids, MI, 1998.

17. C. Peter Wagner. *Breaking Strongholds in Your City.* Regal Books, Ventura, CA, 1993.

18. Derek Prince, *Blessing or Curse: You Can Choose.* Chosen Books, Grand Rapids, MI, 2000.

19. Perry Stone, *Purging Your House, Pruning Your Family Tree. How to rid your home and family of demonic influence and generational oppression.* Charisma House, Mary Lake, FL, 2011.

20. Noel and Phyl Gibson, *Deliver Our Children from the Evil One,* Freedom in Christ Ministries Trust, Drummoyne, NSW, Australia, 1989.

21. Jack Frost. *Experiencing Father's Embrace.* Charisma House, Lake Mary, FL, 2002.

22. Jack Frost. *Experiencing Father's Embrace Workbook.* Father's House Productions, Conway, SC, 2002. www.shilohplace.org.

23. Floyd McClung, Jr. *The Father Heart of God.* Harvest House Publishers. Eugene, Oregon, 1985.

24. Wayne Jacobsen. *He Loves Me*. Windblown Media, Newbury Park, CA, 2007.

25. Henri JM Nouwen. *The Return of the Prodigal Son*. Doubleday, New York, NY, 1992.

26. Henry T. Blackaby and Claude V. King. *Experiencing God*. Broadman & Holman Publishers, Nashville, TN, 1994.

27. Henry T. Blackaby and Claude V. King. *Experiencing God Study Questions*. Broadman & Holman Publishers, Nashville, TN, 1998.

28. Henry T. Blackaby. *Created to Be God's Friend*. Thomas Nelson Publishers, Nashville, TN, 1999.

29. Henry T Blackaby and Roy T. Edgemon. *The Ways of God*. Broadman & Holman Publishers, Nashville, TN, 2000.

30. R.T. Kendall. *A Man After God's Own Heart*. Christian Focus Publications, Ross-shire, UK, 2001.

31. Billy Wilson. *Father Cry*. Chosen Books, Grand Rapids, MI, 2012.

32. Joy Dawson. *Intimate Friendship with God*. Chosen Books, Grand Rapids, MI, 1986.

33. Joy Dawson. *My Journey with Jesus*. Self-published, 11141 Osborne Street, Lake View Terrace, CA 913242, www.JoyDawson.com, 2021.

34. William Paul Young. *The Shack*. Windblown Media, Newbury Park, CA, 2007.

35. William Paul Young. *Cross Roads,* Faith Words, NY, 2012.

36. Trudy Beyak. *The Mother Heart of God,* Faith Word, New York, 2013.

37. Diane Littleton. *The Nurturing God: God's Parenting and Ours.* Self-published, littletondiane@gmail.com, 2016.

38. Francis MacNutt, PhD. *Healing.* Ava Maria Press, Notre Dame, IN, 1974.

39. FF Bosworth. *Christ the Healer.* Whitaker House, New Kensington, PA, 2000.

40. Bill Johnson and Randy Clark. *The Essential Guide to Healing.* Chosen, Minneapolis, 2011.

41. Oral Roberts. *If You Need Healing Do These Things.* Papamoa Press, 2018.

42. Kenneth E. Hagin. *Healing Scriptures.* Faith Library Publications, Tulsa, OK, 1993.

43. John and Paula Sandford. *The Transformation of the Inner Man.* Bridge Publishing, Inc., 1982.

44. John and Paula Sandford. *Healing the Wounded Spirit.* Victory House, Tulsa, OK, 1985.

45. John Sandford and Mark Sanford. *Deliverance and Inner Healing.* Chosen Books, Grand Rapids, MI, 2008.

46. Leanne Payne. *The Broken Image: Restoring Personal Wholeness through Healing Prayer.* Baker Books, Grand Rapids, MI, 1981, 1996.

47. Leanne Payne, *Restoring the Christian Soul: Overcoming Barriers to Completion in Christ Through Healing Prayer.* Baker Books, Grand Rapids, MI, 1991.

48. Carol Peters Tanksley, MD, DMIN. *Overcoming Fear & Anxiety Through Spiritual Warfare.* Charisma House, Lake Mary, FL, 2017.

49. Read more and connect with Dr. Carol Peters-Tanksley at www. drcarolministries.com.

50. Perry Stone, *Exposing Satan's Playbook: The secrets and strategies Satan hopes you never discover.* Charisma House, Mary Lake, FL, 2012.

51. John Eckhardt. *Deliverance and Spiritual Warfare Manual.* Charisma House, Lake Mary, FL, 2014

52. Francis MacNutt. *Deliverance from Evil Spirits: A Practical Manual.* Chosen Books, Grand Rapids, MI, 1995.

53. Leonard Ravenhill. *America Is Too Young to Die.* Bethany Fellowship, Minneapolis, 1979, p. 112

54. John Ankerberg and John Weldon, *The Secret Teachings of the Masonic Lodge.* Moody Publishers, Chicago, 1990.

55. Lester Sumrall, *Demonology & Deliverance, Volume One and Two,* LeSea Publishing, South Bend, IN, 2017.

56. Dutch Sheets, *Watchman Prayer, Protecting Your Family, Home and Community from the Enemy's Schemes.* Chosen Books, Bloomington, MN, 2008.

57. Ronald Know. *Enthusiasm.* Oxford University Press, UK, 1961.

58. Charles Albert Johnson and Ferenc M. Szasz. *The Frontier Camp Meeting.* Southern Methodist University Press, 1955.

59. Charles G. Finney. *Autobiography of Charles G. Finney: A Lifetime of Evangelical Preaching to Christians Across America, Revealed.* Pantianos Classics, 1876.

60. Francis MacNutt, *Overcome by the Spirit.* Chosen Books, Grand Rapids, MI, 1990.

Author's Contact

Donald Tredway: drtreds@aol.com

Donna Tredway: ddtreds@aol.com

www.ingramcontent.com/pod-product-compliance
Lightning Source LLC
Chambersburg PA
CBHW071424090426
42737CB00011B/1561